Basalt and the Frying Pan

Legacy of the Colorado Midland Railroad

Earl V. Elmont

WHO Press • Basalt, Colorado

PUBLISHED BY

WHO Press
0311 West Sopris Creek Road
Basalt, Colorado 81621
www.whopress.com

Library of Congress Control Number: 2004105370

ISBN 1-882426-16-9

Printed in the United States of America

PHOTOGRAPHIC CREDITS

Earl V. Elmont Collection pp. 1,6,18-20, 23,27, 28 (top), 30-31, 33, 35, 39-40, 42, 45, 48-49, 51, 53, 56, 58, 60, 63, 65, 67-72, 75, 77-81, 83-86, 93 (top), 96-97, 99, 101, 103-4, 106, 109, 112-13, 115-19, 121-23, 126 (bottom), 130-31, 133, 135, 137-39, 141-45, 147
Richard Neal Collection pp. 28 (bottom), 89, 92, 93 (bottom), 94-95, 102, 105, 111
Jim Crowley Collection pp. 13, 25, 34, 36, 44, 90-91, 100, 108, 114, 132, 140, 146
Del Gerbaz Collection pp. 16, 22, 26, 29, 37, 66
David La Mont Collection pp. 125, 126 (top)
Wally Dallenbach Collection p. 59
J. Wm. Wells Collection p. 11
Henry Lee Collection p. 54

Cover design by Curt Carpenter
Edited by Warren H. Ohlrich

Table of Contents

Colorado Midland Railroad

Life along the Basalt and Frying Pan Railroad Line

About the Author

Earl Vernon Elmont, named after an uncle, was born in his mother's bed in Basalt on a cold winter's day in January of 1938. After having five sons, his mother wanted a daughter so badly that she cried. However, he was never made to feel unloved or unwanted. On Oct. 3, 1932, Earl's father, Paul Elmont, was terribly injured while working on the Frying Pan auto road about a mile below the current Ruedi Dam. A premature dynamite explosion sent huge chunks of red sandstone flying through the air. Paul Elmont could clearly see the rock coming but could not maneuver his horse team and wagon out of the way. One rock struck him in the thigh while another one knocked the ears off one of the horses. Sudden movement of the injured horse's body pushed Paul's brother, Herbert, into the river. Earl's father was rushed to Porter Hospital in Glenwood. His leg had to be amputated and he walked with crutches the rest of his life.

Times were hard and not everyone in town was well-to-do. Neighbors took pity knowing that Earl's father was severely injured. The game warden brought meat to their home. A local farmer brought milk and potatoes. Earl was offered a meal every time he went to the home of his good friend, Kelvin Arbaney.

Earl was always proud that four of his brothers served in the military. His mother displayed a special flag in her east window with four stars on it. They represented World War II and the Korean conflict. When brothers came home on furlough, the neighbors sent delicious food and cakes for them to enjoy.

Earl attended twelve grades in the Basalt public schools, graduating in 1956 in a class of twelve. He then obtained B.A. and M.A. degrees in colleges in Colorado and Utah. He taught high school subjects such as Spanish, English, Math, Speech and the Holy Scriptures. He traveled with his students in the U.S. and Mexico. With his wife he traveled to Europe and the Middle East. Alone he went to Latin America. Earl speaks Spanish, French and a little German. His paternal grandfather spoke eight languages. Though grandfather was French, his wife was German, so they spoke German in the home. Earl's father never spoke a word of English until he went to first grade in Franklin, Pennsylvania.

Earl and his wife, Claire, are the parents of nine children—six boys and three girls. They currently have thirty-four grandchildren. A couple of his children also speak foreign languages; one speaks Spanish, Italian, Portuguese and English. It seems grandfather made languages come easily to the family.

Mr. Elmont is so obsessed with the Basalt area that he feels compelled to visit it every summer and as often as possible on holidays. It is in his blood. His earlier book, *Basalt, Friendly Town,* is on file in the Basalt Regional Library. In that book, Basalt receives a street by street, house by house consideration.

The author has recently retired after thirty-three years of teaching. He resides in Salt Lake City, Utah. His heart is forever lodged in western Colorado.

Dedication

This book is respectfully dedicated to "Cowboy" Jim Crowley of Thomasville and Rifle, respectively. Jim maintains a winter home in Rifle not too far from his daughter, Betty. He loves to spend much of his summers in his beloved Thomasville, Colorado. There he rents out a trailer and guards the lovely polished-log homes of three of his four children. He helped to build all those homes.

His wife, Eulalia Crowley, is now deceased. He has been a widower for twenty-one years. His brothers were Bud, Ray, and Frank. Frank was one of the men who helped Tucker McClure build railroads, highways and airports in Latin America in the forties. Jim's sisters are Virginia and Marjorie. His children are Lea, Frankie, Jimmy and Betty. Lea is married to John Vasten, formerly of Emma. They live at Thomasville. John used to work for the forest service. Frankie married a coach named Larry Straight and they reside in

Tucson, Arizona. Jimmy married a lady by the name of Audrey and they both work at City Market Pharmacy in El Jebel. Betty married Shane Ortell who specializes in installing window coverings in the Rifle-Silt area.

Jim Crowley was born on October 29th, 1918, in the Porter Hospital in Glenwood Springs. He is currently 86 years old. His father was Claude Crowley, long-time Frying Pan resident, and his mother was Lulu Thompson. The Crowleys first came to the valley from Joplin, Missouri, in 1890, which makes them true pioneers. At the time Claude was only four years old. I still sense a little "Missouri mule" in Jim.

Jim has worked in heavy construction and for a gas company. He also has been a ranch foreman and a businessman. He once owned a hotel and restaurant in Basalt. It was the original hotel and eating house for the Colorado Midland Railroad. Today it is known as the Primavera. Jim also owned the Midland Bar and Café in Basalt.

Jim Crowley possibly deserves the title "Father of the Frying Pan." It is doubtful that anyone else is older who has lived there continuously. No one seems to know the history of the area any better. He has been an invaluable help in the collection of data for this book. He is a veritable "walking encyclopedia." He has the memory, but not the size, of an elephant. His handwriting is atrocious, but what has that got to do with this book? His daughter, Frankie, says it has "....always been bad. We kids used to forge his name to get out of school." We take our hats off to Mr. Gentleman Jim Crowley. This is not the first book to mention him. He is on the front cover of a recent book about cowboys of the Roaring Fork Valley.

Jim is an incredibly tough guy. He has broken his neck twice, which might have killed a lesser man. The last time was in 2002 when he tumbled down an unlighted and unmarked stairway while trying to be a Good Samaritan. He was dropping off used clothing to a charitable organization. The situation became so serious that the doctors summoned his children to come to the hospital to pay their last respects. However, Jim Crowley is no man to mess with. He is still alive and looks as good and tough as ever. He recently experienced a mild heart attack.

The author has grown very fond of the man and is deeply indebted to him. He tried to buy dinner for Mr. Crowley once, but got out-maneuvered and Crowley ended up paying. He has constantly been on the phone providing new and additional information for this book. Not too long ago he provided practically every known cattle brand for every ranch that ever existed on the Frying Pan. How could you not dedicate a book to a man like that?

Preface

The author has an undying love for Basalt and the Frying Pan River Valley. He loves to visit Aspen, Maroon Bells, Independence Pass, Woody Creek, Emma, El Jebel, Carbondale, Marble, and Glenwood Springs. He learned to swim in the Aspen City Pool and spent his childhood swimming in the Glenwood Hot Springs. He worked for Walt Matthews in the Aspen Drug Co.

After his first contact with a Colorado Midland Railway history book, he became obsessed with the little railroad, realizing that his mother once rode on it and participated in its wildflower excursions. After reading other books, he finally bought his first one from a bookstore connected with the railroad depot in Grand Junction, Colorado. From then on he was hooked. He could not get the Midland out of his mind. He has read everything he can get his hands on about the old Colorado Midland. He spent hours wistfully thinking what it would have been like to have ridden the historic little train, passing all its scenic wonders and watching fishermen get off and on as they passed their favorite little fishing holes along the way. He often imagines that he can still hear the whistles blow as he traverses the old railroad bed on the Frying Pan.

His worst realization was that the former books about the Midland were all out of print and, in many cases, the authors were deceased. Who will teach the younger generations about such a rich and colorful legacy? How can the heroic tales of those men and their machines be kept alive? He determined he could not cheat current and future generations out of such a treasure chest of knowledge. His motivation doubled when he realized that he had relatives in every little town and hamlet along the Frying Pan route from Basalt to Norrie and in between. He owed it to them to "speak from the dust" (of history) once again.

The author feels the job would not be done to speak only of the railroad. Dozens of warm and untold human interest stories can be found in every little hamlet along the Frying Pan route. It is with the worthy goal in mind of bringing alive the stories and history along this route that the author has produced this volume for what he hopes will be rich and rewarding reading for all, not just for those fortunate enough to have lived on the Frying Pan River shores.

The effort has been long and painstaking, but worth the time and cost. Neophyte that he is, the author has accepted help wherever he could find it. Revising, correcting, changing, improving the book has been a most arduous task but, anything worth doing is worth doing well. If the book has weaknesses, they are his. If it has errors, the author is mortal. If it has strengths, it is due to people like the publisher, Mr. Warren Ohlrich of Basalt.

The author wishes hours of pleasant reading and happy memories for older generations. For younger ones he hopes the book brings an increased appreciation for living in such a peaceful and scenic setting as Basalt and its environs.

Acknowledgments

I must thank Jim Crowley, first of all, for taking me many places I needed to visit in researching this book. He told me many stories I never knew about the Frying Pan Valley. He was present as a twelve-year-old boy the day my father was terribly injured while working on the Frying Pan auto road. Jim's father, Claude Crowley, was the foreman on the work crew the day of the accident.

I also want to acknowledge dad's attempts to provide for me and five other siblings as long as he could. It wasn't easy. He prospected for gold on Basalt Mountain but never found any. He even sold pencils door to door to keep food on the table. There were neither penicillin nor good antibiotics in those days. Gangrene set in and dad finally succumbed in August of 1941. How his dignity must have suffered! This young Pennsylvania man came to eastern Colorado to dry farm. The "Dust Bowl" drove him out, and then to end up in such an ignoble way trying to make the one-time railroad bed into a decent auto road. We all cried when we read his death certificate years later. "Death due in part to a lifetime of poverty." My, how fortunate we younger generations seem to be!

We thank our mother's people who also came to Colorado early enough to qualify us as "pioneers." The Hennings and the Jakemans came from Iowa. Jakeman Creek, near Thomasville, is named for our maternal grandfather.

Next I must thank my old high school buddy, Darol Woolley, of Basalt. He once lived on the Cap-K Ranch at Sloss. He and Mr. Joe Gregg, Jr. told me much about that area. Darol was the first to tell me about an old abandoned Chinese village near the Mallon Tunnel and Jim Crowley was the first to take me there. The Chinese were cooks for the Midland and also helped to lay the rails. If the Forest Service is correct, the existence of this village has only come to light recently.

The author seems to be part of a small minority of people who have ever toured the fabled Tucker McClure home at Sloss. For this he is indebted to that gregarious and affable Joe Gregg, Jr. Joe's father and Mr. Miller Nichols purchased the extensive Tucker McClure properties. Mr. Gregg gave the author an extensive two-hour tour of the place and then invited me to investigate the old county road, the High Line. At a point slightly above Cap-K Ranch the road crossed the river over to the south side and continued there until the site of the current Ruedi Dam. If one peers through the trees carefully, he can still see what looks like an old road in the trees and brush on the south side.

I must thank my wife, Claire, for believing in me and for tolerating my absences while I tramped the hills of my beloved Colorado photographing place after place. My brother, Cliff, was a big help to me in gathering materials for this book; so was my brother, Fred. My twin cousins, Ruth and Alice Vagneur, lent moral support and encouraged me. My aunt, Linda Arlian Nelson, not only loaned me her home as a base for writing the book but also her food. She wishes she and her sisters, Palmyra Favre and Jennie Arlian, had written a book similar to the one that sisters, Mary and Martha (Waterman) recently published called "Sis." Linda could have related topics from Woody Creek to El Jebel.

I must not forget that undaunting Patricia (Hyrup) Yale of Buena Vista for all the help she sent me about the Hyrups. Her grandfather, Jens Peter Hyrup, was one of the first engineers in the valley to work for the Midland. Her father and mother, Chris and Hazel Hyrup, ranched on the Frying Pan before moving to Basalt. Her uncle, Walter Hyrup, was one of the most prominent men in Basalt, having worked for the railroad and having served as town marshal. He was a story-teller "par excellence."

Mr. Whit McClelland of Florida was a big help in matters of publication. He is the man who remodeled Swede's Garage in 1969 back to its original Midland Depot condition. It is now the Alpine Bank in Basalt.

Mr. Warren Ohlrich, of WHO Press in Basalt, answered my prayers while searching for a publisher. When I almost gave up hope, here he came on his white charger and rescued my efforts from despair. I thoroughly trust this talented and capable man.

Introduction

As an author I have fallen in love with the stories of the old Colorado Midland Railroad. Its route began in Colorado Springs and climbed its way westward through many a picturesque little town, over many difficult mountain passes, through gorges and fifteen tunnels until it reached the busiest little silver town in the West, Leadville. From there it entered three more tunnels as it pierced the backbone of the mighty Rockies, leaving Lake County and entering Pitkin and Eagle counties. At one time in its history it had the highest broad-gauge track in the country and, perhaps, the highest trestle. The Midland forced other railroads to display their competitive edge and switch to broad-gauge also. It raced its way into that other silver capital, Aspen, against the mighty Denver and Rio Grande (D&RG), losing the race by only a month or so. Big in aspirations and high on dreams, it extended itself all the way to Salt Lake City, Utah, and beyond, sharing a track with the D&RG from New Castle westward. It was hungry for silver and coal found in other states.

In the beginning the railroad was the life-blood of Basalt, but the ending of the Colorado Midland was not so happy. I have earned an undying respect for Mr. Albert Carlton, for whom the main tunnel through the Continental Divide was named when it became an auto road after the collapse of the railroad in 1918. No one struggled more valiantly to keep the little railroad alive and to respect its workers than he did. The U. S. government must take the main blame

for the demise of the embattled little railroad when it "nationalized" all rail lines as a safety measure during WWI. In the process it favored the D&RG with the bulk of shipments and the little Midland slipped into history.

Basalt, like its big sister Aspen, experienced a slump. As big sister arose in the 1950s and became one of the world's foremost ski centers, Basalt arose with it as a bedroom community. People all up and down the Roaring Fork and Frying Pan valleys, who learned the value of knuckle-busting hard work, now began to sell their agriculture-related enterprises. They soon saw their lands converted to uses more akin to the ski industry. In the process many people became quite wealthy.

The fishing industry shifted into high gear in the fifties and sixties on both rivers, as well as on the Crystal in Carbondale. Basalt became a fisherman's and a tourist's paradise. People from Arkansas, Oklahoma, Texas and elsewhere were drawn back to Basalt summer after summer. Their arrival was as sure a thing as the arrival of the vernal equinox. Building booms continued and the basic nature of little Basalt changed in many ways that would not be recognizable to the "old timers."

As Basalt changed, so did the surrounding valleys, including the Frying Pan. It appeared that there were two types of lucky people—those who hung onto their lands from the earliest days and did not have to pay exorbitant prices as a "spillover" from Aspen's price tags, and those who were wealthy enough to buy a piece of land on which to build a home, ranch or resort. Some of us, caught in the "middle", have been forever envious.

This book wishes to dwell on human interest stories as much as on the Midland Railroad. The best human interest stories came from old-timers like Jim Crowley, to whom this book is dedicated. The next best source was from illustrious men who moved in and were true "movers and shakers" like Tucker McClure, Peter Jouflas, Dr. John Schweppe and the well-known race car driver, Wally Dallenbach. It appears that the Frying Pan Valley is evolving from a place of beauty and a sportsman's paradise to a famous place. People like the singers Neil Diamond and John Denver, and the famous drummer, Ringo Starr, helped to make it that way.

Is the Colorado Midland gone? Yes! Forgotten? Never! Not as long as mother's blood flows in my veins and the memory of her, on shopping trips on the Midland and on wildflower excursions, remains in my heart. What I wouldn't give for one day on the old Midland, doing what so many liked to do—Breakfast in Leadville. Lunch in Basalt or Aspen and home again in time for dinner. Although the Colorado Midland has been gone for almost 100 years, its legacy still lives on.

The Colorado Midland Railroad

The Founders

Getting Started

The two hundred and sixty-one mile Midland route was started by Mr. Homer D. Fisher, the major promoter. Most of the activity in Rocky Mountain railroading started around Colorado Springs. Fisher asked Wm. A. Bell to help him. Bell agreed but, for some strange reason, Bell was never allowed to be anything more than a stockholder. Perhaps it was Bell's personal wish.

Henry T. Rogers, a Denver banker, was invited to join the corporation. Thomas Wigglesworth signed on too. He was a railroad "locating engineer." Edwin W. Edwards of Colorado Springs became the very first president. Together, these men incorporated the Midland Railroad on November 23, 1883. At this time there was railroad activity all over America and, ever since the transcontinental railroad was completed in Utah in 1869, the railroad fever was evident in Colorado.

Colorado Midland Railway ascends Hagerman Pass on the east side of the Continental Divide. The great Horshoe Trestle supports the second loop down the mountainside.

Two different railroad tunnels were to pierce the Rockies. The first was the Hagerman Tunnel at 11,500 feet in elevation. Sixteen miles west of Leadville, it pierced the heart of the Saguache Range and allowed the Midland to drop into the Frying Pan River Valley. The second was the Busk-Ivanhoe Tunnel, much lower in elevation and five times longer.

Because of the distance from Leadville to Basalt and the presence of the intervening Continental Divide, the railroad's construction was considered to be one of the greatest engineering feats in all of America. At one time, the Midland Railroad boasted of being the highest broad-gauge line in America and in all the world. Cutting through places like Hell Gate was a masterful feat indeed. Crossing all the gullies on the eastern side was no small feat either, nor was the building of the snow sheds and all the smaller little tunnels. If the two main tunnels were numbers 16A (Hagerman) and 16B (Busk-Ivanhoe), then there were fifteen more tunnels on the eastern side and one more (Mallon) on the western side for a total of eighteen tunnels. Wow! Some of the eastern ones were incredibly close to one another and, in at least one spot, one could see daylight through four of them at a time.

Hagerman

James J. Hagerman, for whom the shorter tunnel was named, as well as the pass that now bypasses the tunnels over to Leadville, came west from Michigan and Minnesota suffering from tuberculosis. This same malady brought more than one entrepreneur west. Hagerman's doctor had predicted that the clean crisp pure mountain air would heal him. In Hagerman's case, the doctor was right. In Mr. Albert Carlton's case, (whom we'll hear more about later), it only helped for a while and he eventually succumbed to the dreadful malady. This is what also killed my father's first wife from Pennsylvania. Earlier, before Hagerman got involved, the upper tunnel was called the Saguache. The name was changed to Hagerman when he became president of the Midland Railroad.

Hagerman was not the least interested in railroading at first. He was a minerals and precious metals man. He had mines in Michigan and smelters in Minnesota and owned vast deposits of iron ore in upper Michigan. He no sooner settled in Colorado Springs, where he built himself a sumptuous mansion, then he bought into the Mollie Gibson Mine at Aspen. He also wasted no time in buying coal fields in Garfield County. He became acquainted with the famous Jerome Wheeler and they had multiple dealings together. He was interested in Aspen's silver wealth and the coal around Glenwood Springs. He was, no doubt, around when the largest chunk of silver ever mined came out of the Smuggler Mine in Aspen. It weighed 1,825 pounds.

As famous as Aspen was in those days, with the most tenacious merchants who found wealth by "hanging on" when other communities folded one by one, Leadville holds the record for producing the most vast amounts of silver in the world's history. It also produced lead, gold and zinc. It was the most bustling little mining town you ever saw in the late 1800s. I love to go there to visit today and shop in its quaint little stores. I can still smell history in the air while walking those little streets. I can shut my eyes and imagine that I just saw "Unsinkable Molly Brown" or Baby Doe Tabor walk by. I shudder to recollect that Baby Doe died penniless in Leadville living in or near her mine shaft.

By June of 1885 Hagerman was already president of the Midland Railroad and ordered the extension of the Midland Line to Aspen and clear to Salt Lake City, Utah. That may be difficult for some of you to believe and may come as a complete surprise. Hagerman was interested in Utah's vast coal deposits and the silver from Alta, Utah, and other places. He even built a branch line southward in Utah from a small place known as Thistle clear to Manti, Richfield and Marysvale. He had a branch line running from Emma, near Basalt, to coal fields in the mountains southwest of there. His line also picked up silver from the famous Park City, headquarters of the recent Winter Olympics, and extended on to Ogden, a city famous on the Union Pacific line. Hagerman eventually canceled many of the little branch lines.

Busk & Carlton

James R. Busk, for whom the lower tunnel is partly named, and for whom the small town on the east end of the tunnel was named, was a wealthy retired merchant from the New York area. Both Hagerman and Rogers, the Denver banker, convinced Busk to invest. Albert E. Carlton, for whom the Busk-Ivanhoe Tunnel was renamed in the early twenties after it became an auto road, and his younger brother, Leslie, came west without any money to speak of. They came from Illinois in 1889 just as things were starting to go well and starting to produce some revenue. They made their money the hard way by selling mining supplies and wagons, and engaging in shipping. As the eastern area of the mountains grew, so did their fortunes. Soon they too were buying into railroads. Albert, like Mr. Hagerman before him, suffered from tuberculosis. He had the more pleasant personality of the two Carltons, but Leslie was the real businessman.

The Carltons came onto the scene rather late. They are most famous for their valiant efforts to try to save the little railroad in the days of its decline. When the line was finally closed in 1918, but took a few more years to really die out, (and longer than that on the eastern side), the Carltons salvaged much of their fortune by selling engines, rails and scrap metals. Some of their engines were sold back East, in the West and as far away as old Mexico.

Albert Carlton has won the author's undying respect. He was the best boss the railroad ever had. He was much more personable than his brother. One time he traveled the entire length of his railroad and shook the hand of every single employee on duty, which amounted to over two thousand people. It was obvious how much he cared for the little railroad and how sad he was when it died. He was honest to a fault. When thefts of gold ore, supplies and wages began to occur on the Midland, Carlton was forced to pay salaries by check instead of valuable ore. If ever a man was to be admired in Colorado railroading, it was Albert E. Carlton.

Tunnels Into The Frying Pan

Tunnel Building

In tunnel building it was always the practice to start on both ends and work toward the middle. When they did that in ancient Jerusalem on the famous Hezekiah's Tunnel, they were amazed that, with their crude techniques, they ended up one yard from each other in the middle and could hear each other's voices. The Busk-Ivanhoe people did better than that, working with much better instruments. They ended up 2 ½ inches out of line from one another. It is amazing what advanced tools they employed on this longer of the two tunnels. The Ingersoll Company had created fabulous and durable drills (diamond bits, perhaps?). They had air compressors and water hoses in the tunnels. There was a system for pumping out foul air and for excess water. They even had power plants outside the tunnels which provided electricity for long strings of lights used inside the tunnels to help the workers see.

Hagerman Tunnel

Preliminary work first started on the Frying Pan side of the mountain in April, 1886. When they first attempted to begin work on the west side of the

Colorado Midland Telegraph & Train Order Office at West Portal of Hagerman Tunnel. Elevation 11,528'. Highest station on the railroad. April, 1899.

Hagerman Tunnel, there were no roads. They had to pack all their materials and supplies over the mountain by pack mule. It is definitely ingenious how they got some of their heaviest supplies over the mountain. They created huge swinging log booms that were anchored to big pine trees by strong cables. These booms swung materials over gullies and high ridges. In like manner, materials that were too heavy for the mules, such as 60- and 90-pound rails, were swung over the mountains by these booms. Like hundreds or thousands of over-sized ants, they worked to complete the seemingly impossible. Wouldn't they be completely amazed and awe-struck at some of our clover-leaf highway interchanges today and some of our enormous skyscrapers, not to mention our trains, planes, automobiles, ships and bridges?

Actual construction began on the east end of the tunnel three weeks before the west end. This was due to easier access to supplies on the eastern side coming from Leadville and Colorado Springs. By this time, quite a good trail had been constructed over the top of the mountain to the west side of Hagerman. Things must have moved quickly after that because by summer of 1887 they were delivering mail to John Ruedi in the hamlet named after him.

The mountain above Hagerman Tunnel was only about five hundred feet higher than the tunnel itself. The tunnel once was the highest railroad point on the entire Midland route and one of the highest in the nation. I would imagine that the old line from Chamas, New Mexico, into Naturita, Colorado, might possibly rival the Midland for elevation. The tunnel took the railroad higher even than the much heralded line between Durango and Silverton.

Busk-Ivanhoe Tunnel

Mr. Michael Keefe and Company of Butte, Montana, which has always been so ugly from mining tailings that the locals have called it "butt", was hired to build the lower tunnel. Mr. Busk was an important railroad man from the eastern slope of the Rockies. So they named a small construction camp after him right at the eastern entrance to the tunnel. The tunnel was under construction by 1891. The Ivanhoe end started two months before the eastern Busk end. It was strongly believed by all that a lower tunnel would solve a myriad of problems. With the project only a thousand feet from completion, (remember, this tunnel is five times longer than the Hagerman Tunnel), Mr. Keefe got terribly sick and dropped out of the project. It was left to the tunnel owners to find a way to finish the job.

A pump house was sorely needed on the Ivanhoe end. Both ends needed power plants, compressor stations, steam plants, extra spur lines, construction buildings, offices and sleeping and eating quarters for the workers. Three great water pumps were needed on the western side. They could extract one hundred to three hundred gallons of water per minute in case such was needed to keep the workers safe. We cannot emphasize enough how dangerous work was in some parts of the tunnel. Soft dirt had to be immediately timbered. In the most dangerous places double timbering had to be installed. One of the biggest headaches of all was clearing debris from the tunnels. Small five-ton locomotives ran on twenty-inch tracks pulling several loaded dump cars or "tram" cars. Outside, immense piles of rubble built up.

They had electric lights to enable them to see inside the tunnels. They were peculiar looking, indeed. Imagine a giant string of old-fashioned white

The piles of rubble taken from inside the Hagerman Tunnel.

Christmas tree lights with larger sized cords and bigger bulbs running into the tunnel from an outside power source.

When trains finally ran through the tunnel on a regular basis, they were not only required to have a giant headlight on but, also, to ring their bell all the way through the tunnel.

In 1892 the tunnel was progressing at a very slow rate with problems cropping up continually. During one period of construction a massive cave-in caused the deaths of thirty Chinese workers. The Chinese were usually the main cooks for the construction crews and they also worked on the roadbeds and the rails. Since no earlier book ever mentioned this unfortunate disaster, how do we verify it? Well, Walter Hyrup, of Basalt, was a railroad worker. His father, Jens Peter Hyrup, was an engineer. Peter told Walter about it and Walter told his son, Johnny. We can't get much better than that. Johnny says they didn't know where most of the workers came from nor who their next of kin were, so they pulled the bodies out of the rubble and buried them in the muddy shores of Lake Ivanhoe. These workers are most likely the people who built the Chinese village directly above the old Mallon Tunnel, a mile or two below Hell Gate. If one can find the caved-in Mallon Tunnel and hikes due north of it, he will find the remains of ten or twelve old cabins, two barns, a mess hall and an ice house for keeping food. It is well worth the hike. Mallon Creek runs right through the middle of the place and, amazingly enough, the workers drank out of Mallon Creek daily with no ill effects.

This was not the only tragedy to have happened during the construction of this lower tunnel. A boy was killed when he tripped carrying a box of blasting powder. A sudden water source flushed one man practically clear out of the tunnel. Huge pumps were needed to constantly drain the tunnel of unwanted water. Fans were used to remove polluted airs when trains began coursing through the tunnel while workers were still engaged inside. Some passed out from the foul air and had to be rushed to the exit. At least one man died in there before he could reach fresh air. Other men were injured or killed from sudden rock cave-ins.

The Busk-Ivanhoe Tunnel, unlike its sister Tunnel, the Hagerman, needed constant shoring up with logs known as "timbers." A weak stone known as "talc" caused a constant headache. In other parts of the tunnel huge cave openings caused the builders headaches, since they did not know how to build a roof under such a massive opening. (Kind of like trying to shore up Carlsbad Caverns.) A few of the workers became quite concerned, not knowing what they would find next in their drilling.

The temperature outside the tunnel never climbed above the low eighties all that summer. Imagine how wet and damp the working conditions must have been inside the tunnel! A typical mountain cave maintains a standard temperature of somewhere around 58 degrees inside winter and summer.

The tunnel was finally finished in August of 1893. The station outside of the tunnel was the first train station ever built on the entire Frying Pan. The crew on the eastern Busk side was 500 feet ahead of the crew on the west side. Estimates of the final cost of construction were well over a million dollars, not counting the loss of precious lives. The first train through the tunnel traveled from east to west on December 13, 1893. That meant construction took a little

West end of the Ivanhoe Tunnel today.

over two years. When the trains started coming through, the Ivanhoe depot moved closer to the tunnel entrance. It had been well out by mid-lake closer to the original dam for the man-made lake, along with a water tank and a fairly large snowshed.

Comparison Of The Two Tunnels

The builders of the Hagerman Tunnel were much more fortunate than those of the Busk-Ivanhoe. The former encountered mostly stable granite while the latter experienced various types of rock, caves, water deposits, "talc", mud and other headaches. Hagerman was the source of some silver and some lead. Busk-Ivanhoe produced nothing in the way of mineral riches. Hagerman had to "timber" only the two openings, while Busk had to shore up many places. This caused many frequent delays and headaches. The Hagerman Tunnel was built for a mere two hundred thousand dollars. The longer one cost a million before it was through.

The upper tunnel was referred to as the "high line" and required an extra six miles of track up the west mountain to reach it. The Hagerman had very

Timbers in the west end of the Hagerman Tunnel.

fancy stone carved entrances chiseled by a man from Colorado City near Colorado Springs. The lower tunnel had wooden portals on both ends which also served as snowsheds. This lower tunnel required massive fans to help blow the acrid smoke out of the tunnel faster. The upper tunnel had at least one snowshed on each end and three more on the west before reaching Ivanhoe. The upper tunnel had nine snowsheds on the east side of the mountain and massive bridges. The Horseshoe Trestle, and at least one showshed, were record holders for size and/or length. The snowshed was 2,110 feet long. The great Horseshoe Trestle, an engineering marvel, was four stories high and 1,084 feet long with numerous vertical supports in at least one hundred different places along its length. When the Horseshoe Trestle (on the second big loop down the mountainside on the eastern slope) was being built, it required a fairly sizeable tent city to be built below it to house the workers. Hundreds of laborers worked and lived there. Those who love to trek those mountains today, who are part thrill-seekers, love to look for old relics of the once great trestle as it lies in ruins on the valley floor below.

The Leadville citizens made jokes when the Ivanhoe Tunnel opened. They all swore that the velocity of the winds had increased. The lower tunnel was much more straight than the upper one and on a clear day, a person could actually "see the light at the end of the tunnel", a distance of nearly two miles. When trains were in the Ivanhoe Tunnel, it became very dangerous for the track workers. The air became noxious and deadly. The Busk end of the tunnel was 134 feet lower than the Ivanhoe end. This helped to create a natural draft that swept the tunnel free of foul smoke in about an hour's time. Even then, many workers were sickened by the foul air. Many a man had to rush for the exit. Some passed out from the fumes who could not make it in time, and at least one man died. Sometimes, even passengers exited the tunnel as dirty as if they had just toured a coal mine. This problem lessened when the potent fumes produced by coal became the more compatible fumes produced by coke. Some coal, by nature, burns much cleaner and better than other types. Coke gave a real boost to the engines also as it burned hotter and better.

Outside the tunnel, Ivanhoe had a depot, three toilets, a pump house, a section house, a bunk house, a handcar house, sheep pens, a 75-ton coal bin, a "wye" for turning engines, a water tank, a long snowshed away from the tunnel and, later, a round house brought down from Hagerman.

Demise Of The Colorado Midland

Competition with the D&RG

As the Midland ran along on its broad-gauge line, the Denver and Rio Grande paralleled it in many places on its narrow-gauge line in the east. Diverging at Leadville, the Midland took its Basalt route and the D&RG went through Eagle county to Glenwood Springs. Again they competed to Aspen. The Midland ran down the Snowmass side of the river and the D&RG traversed the Woody Creek side.

In 1887 the race into the mining town of Aspen by the two railroads was won by the D&RG by three months. The bridge the Midland constructed across Maroon Creek outside of Aspen was one of the reasons that the D&RG. beat the Midland into Aspen. Metal materials arrived late from the east and that huge bridge was delayed. Meanwhile, the D&RG moved merrily on its way into Aspen on the easier Woody Creek side of the Roaring Fork River. The

Colorado Midland freight crossing the Maroon Creek bridge approaching Aspen in about 1888.

Castle Creek bridge, closer to Aspen, also caused the Midland another delay.

My mother told an exciting story about the Maroon Creek bridge. She happened to be on the train in about 1915. The train suddenly stopped in the middle of that awesome bridge. The engineer began to toot his whistle repeatedly. Finally, mother opened a window and poked her head out just in time to see a full-grown cow plunge to her death off the bridge. I know mother wouldn't have lied. Apparently the approaches to the bridge had no cattle guards, which would have scared the hapless critter away. The bridge must have had solid boards so that people on foot could have crossed it. The cow ventured onto the bridge and, when the engineer scared it, it became "ground beef."

Financial Problems

The tunnels became an expensive problem. A dispute broke out over custody of the precious metals in the Hagerman. Did they belong to the railroad corporate directors or to the workers who found them? A court finally settled the dispute ruling in favor of the corporate leaders. No minerals were found in the lower Busk Tunnel.

The railroad did not own the lower tunnel; another corporation belonging to its builders did. The Midland had to lease the lower tunnel for 25¢ per passenger and 25¢ per head of livestock. This became shocking to the Midland owners when they totaled up a year's lease and it was $90,000 dollars or more. They used this lower expensive tunnel for four years before switching back to the upper "high line" route for nearly two years. To solve the problem, the Midland eventually bought the Busk-Ivanhoe Tunnel for millions of dollars and closed the Hagerman Tunnel once and for all. Not long after, the Midland tore out the upper tracks and all those incredible trestles.

Boarding the Colorado Midland in Basalt in 1915.

The Terrible Winter Of 1899

The poor Midland Railroad had plenty of troubles of its own without Mother Nature venting her furies. In January of 1899 it snowed thirty-five feet deep at Hagerman Tunnel (altitude: 11,500 feet). In spite of the efforts of over 150 "snowbirds" (shovelers), the railroad refused to be dug out and it came to a complete standstill. Passengers and workers, merchandise and livestock, on both sides of the Saguache Range, were trapped. Some snowsheds on the eastern side collapsed, blocking the entire route. One large snowshed collapsed on a freight train loaded with livestock. The animals all froze to death before help could arrive.

From dripping water and lack of use for four years, ice twelve inches thick formed on the rails inside the tunnel. The tunnel was nearly half a mile long and men had to use sledge hammers to remove the ice. Trains, people and stations all became marooned. They were cut off from society for 77 days, from January until April. Supplies and food were delivered on foot to the various little stations with the help of men on snowshoes. Fortunately, enough coal was on hand that people kept warm, even in the engines. Wherever possible, engineers hiked to a local station. At times the snow would slightly melt and then refreeze the next night, becoming solid ice. In this case the snowbirds had to use dynamite to free the tracks.

Various types of snow plows were used in a valiant attempt to free the trains. Giant rotary blades were brought in from Chicago. The blades on the rotary were nine feet long, but were of no avail. Auger-type plows were brought in and, with the help of the spring thaw, the little line finally escaped confinement. At least one station master at Ivanhoe committed suicide shortly after he was freed from his wintry confinement. The snow got so deep at that station that they couldn't use the front door. The back door was on a steep incline, so it was easier to keep free from snow. However, yet unknown trials and tribulations awaited this first broad gauge line to ever pierce the Rockies.

The terrible winter of 1899 forced them back to the lower tunnel. Now they decided they had better purchase it. The high line was then dismantled forever and the roundtable was moved down to the Ivanhoe side of the lower tunnel. They had formerly used a "wye" to reroute trains. By June of 1899, with the terrible winter snows now melted, trains were running smoothly through the Busk-Ivanhoe, and the Hagerman Tunnel passed into history.

Midland Railroad Ownership and Receivership

Ten days after the first train ran through the Busk-Ivanhoe Tunnel, the Midland Railroad and its parent company, the Santa Fe Railroad, went into financial receivership. This meant that if someone didn't do something very quickly, the railroad would be bankrupt and would revert to the hands of the creditors. On October 11, 1897, The Colorado Midland Railroad became the Colorado Midland RAILWAY Company. What a non-distinct, subtle little name change! This suggested new ownership.

The longest any one organization controlled the Colorado Midland Railroad was eleven years. Four different men and/or companies became receivers during the Midland's financial distresses. First was the Santa Fe Railroad. Second was a Mr. Ristine. Third was Mr. Vallery, whose name once appeared on every little printed detail of the railroad from freight invoices to free passes. Fourth was the famous Mr. Albert Carlton who tried harder than anyone else, in the author's opinion, to save the struggling little enterprise. Mr. Carlton could not have known at the time of his purchase that the little line only had months left to live.

Tearing up rails and yards in Basalt, likely in January, 1921.

The railroad experienced four different name changes during its life span. First it was the Midland Railway Company. Then it was simply the Midland Railroad. Next it was the Midland Railway again and, finally, the Midland Railroad a second time. Though it may not have officially received the following designation, it was once called by the common people "The Santa Fe Midland." Seven different railroad companies owned or controlled it: Mr. Hagerman and the Colorado Midland; Santa Fe Railroad; Rio Grande Western; Colorado and Southern; Denver and Rio Grande; Chicago Burlington and Quincy; U. S. Railroad Administration during WW I.

In August of 1918 all the Midland's troubles combined into one massive Excedrin headache to deliver a final "coup de grace" to the valiant little railroad. In another year or so, all the rails were removed and the little line passed silently into history.

Car #100, "Cascade", being moved from Colorado Springs to a location 2 miles north of the Woody Creek siding. 1950.

Vestiges Of The Colorado Midland

Hagerman Tunnel

The upper Hagerman Tunnel, unlike the Busk-Ivanhoe below it, once had a fancy carved stone entrance on each side of the Continental Divide. A man from Colorado City came up there and carved both entrances out of solid granite found naturally on the Saguache Mountain Range. The lower tunnel only had wooden entrances, which were really more like snowsheds, on both sides of the mountain.

The eastern end of the Hagerman Tunnel today is constantly filled with four or five feet of ice. It seldom, if ever, sees the sunshine long enough to melt it. The west end, however, freezes five or six feet deep in the winter and thaws completely every summer. Brave-hearted men, or foolish (I don't know which), may try to venture into the west end. A friend of mine hopes to take a boat in there to skim past the watery part and explore the solid granite in the rest of the tunnel. The author has no knowledge whatever as to the condition of the inside of the Hagerman Tunnel. There are those who believe it is still passable, but the author does not recommend it and I am sure state authorities would not look upon such an endeavor favorably. Besides, there could be a mountain lion holed up in there.

Darol Woolley, of Basalt, prepares to enter the west portal of Hagerman Tunnel with his car battery-operated flashlight.

Water emerges from the east side of Busk-Ivanhoe Tunnel, later called the Carlton Tunnel.

Hagerman was unlike Busk-Ivanhoe in that it was pretty solid all the way through. Busk-Ivanhoe had all sorts of tricky soil, cave-ins, natural caves, water deposits, etc. It was much more a headache for the builders than the upper tunnel was. Landslides, either natural or man-made, seem to block both the entrance and the exit to both tunnels.

There is no use whatever today for the Hagerman Tunnel. When its rails were taken up and its buildings, including the roundhouse, were moved after the big winter of 1899, that was the end of the practical use of the Hagerman, or the high line, forever. Mr. J. J. Hagerman's name still thrives today in the form of Hagerman Pass which goes from Lake Ivanhoe over to Leadville and vicinity. I do not recommend this route for a nice passenger car in any way, shape or form. I would use a jeep or a four-wheel drive truck with heavy duty tires. Though the top of the pass was beautiful and the view of Lake Ivanhoe from up there was exquisite, I have never bounced around so much on any pass in my life and hope to never do it again. In mid July we found snow banks two and three times taller than our pickup truck that had been sliced through by the road crews.

Carlton Tunnel

Whereas the Hagerman Tunnel required shoring up or timbering only at the entrance and the exit, the Busk-Ivanhoe required the same throughout much of its nearly two-mile length. It was five times longer than its earlier upper rival. The Busk-Ivanhoe, later named the Carlton Tunnel when it became an auto tunnel and part of a highway, is caved in throughout much of the tunnel, including the middle. Quite a sum of money was spent in the fifties to turn the Busk-

West end of Carlton Tunnel. 1940s.

Ivanhoe into a water diversion tunnel as part of the Frying Pan-Arkansas diversion project. Though one cannot see water coming out of Lake Ivanhoe and flowing into the tunnel, it is clearly seen coming out the eastern side where it joins the water shed that flows into Turquoise Lake. Somehow the water makes its way to both Pueblo and Aurora, Colorado. I am sure that thirsty Denver uses all it can get, but I have heard that Pueblo occasionally leases its excess flow to thirsty consumers along the route. The Arkansas River on the eastern slope does its part in keeping the water moving along.

When Albert E. Carlton donated his tunnel to the state as an auto tunnel, the name was changed to Carlton Tunnel in his honor. My brother had the privilege of riding through it before it caved in during the 1940s. He was with his good friend, Bus Arbaney, and two lovely girls. When they emerged from the east end, they were black and wet with soot that had leaked down from the ceiling in many places. It is no wonder they ended up closing it. It's too bad they went through in a convertible. Autos going east went through on the hour and those going west on the half hour. Since it only took twenty minutes to traverse the tunnel, that left ten minutes of grace time to avoid accidents. One lady had car trouble in the middle of the tunnel. After much difficulty and after causing much frustration for fellow travelers, she finally emerged saying: "Don't think I wasn't trying to get my a _ _ out of there!"

Del Gerbaz standing by the clock used to control traffic though the Carlton Tunnel, 1932. Tunnel was closed to auto traffic in 1933.

Laundry Trains and Wildflower Excursions

At times the Denver and Rio Grande and the Midland became highly competitive. This was great for the consumer! Sometimes the going rate for a weekend trip to Glenwood and back from Aspen was a dollar-and-a-half. As the competition increased, a free dip in the Glenwood Pool was offered. Since people had to take a swim suit, a towel and a possible change of clothing in case the first one got wet, the trains became known as "laundry trains." Occasionally these trips were offered "gratis" just to out-do the other railroad company.

For a dollar-and-a-half, a person could also go on a wildflower excursion from Leadville to Basalt. People often packed lunches. I don't recall if the train waited for them to pick their flowers or if it met them on the return trip from somewhere in the valley. It may seem a little unusual for us today with our televisions and our fast cars and our video cameras, that some past generation would get joy out of a wildflower excursion. But I think it is a delightful idea. My mother went on many of them before the railroad went out in 1918 at just about the time she married.

With life on the Colorado plains, as a married woman near Byers, she had no time for wildflower excursions any more. There were babies to tend, chickens to feed, hay to stack and many other mundane chores. Even a trip to the nearest mailbox was no picnic. Mother invariably found a rattle-snake guarding her mail box. One time she threw her shoe at it and it refused to move. On another day she carried her six-shooter along with her. The rattler coiled as she approached it. My brothers remarked to their dying day what a good shot mother was. She plugged that old rattler three times; when dad lifted it up, it had six bullet holes in it. That will teach a rattlesnake not to coil!

Blanche Elmont, 1945.

Thank goodness for a national farmers' organization called the Grange, or mother may have had little social life at all. As her sister, Maude, once complained: "I'm a mountain girl (Norrie) and here I am stuck out on the plains." Mother must have felt the same. After 1932 they got their wish to go back to their beloved mountains.

During the wildflower excursions, one could count in the old photos as many as 150 or more persons, both men and women. There were also some children. In photos showing the least amount of people, perhaps twenty-five were pictured. Each person had a complete armful of flowers. I have often mused that the hills must have been bare of flowers (like a plague of locusts going through). But, fortunately, flowers do drop seeds and there always seemed to be a gorgeous carpet of fresh flowers each spring. Surely, Mother Nature should have won the Good Housekeeping Seal of Approval. I recall that my mother could just about name every flower on the Frying Pan. I suppose some expert was along on the trains on the original excursions teaching every-one the names of the flowers. In modern times an aunt of mine served as a guide at a famous tourist spot in Illinois. There were at least 150 different flowers growing out in the yard of her particular little historic home. She amazed me that she knew the name of every single one of the flowers. Mother had that same knowledge about the flowers on the Frying Pan.

A professional photographer always went along on the excursions. It was popular to climb all over the train, particularly the engine, holding on with one hand while grasping the coveted flowers in the other, while one's picture was snapped. The photographer would go back to the point of origin and develop the pictures and one could call on him a week or so later or have the photo mailed for a certain price. The picture arrived in a neat little "folio."

Occasionally a second train was required to handle all those interested in an excursion. Some of the cars were covered but others were open-aired. The view of the countryside was terrific from one of those open cars. The fresh mountain air was invigorating. How often I have wished they would reopen the rail line from Glenwood to Aspen!

The Colorado Midland had one or more musical bands operating at all times. They offered frequent concerts in Colorado Springs and elsewhere as they were able. They performed at important public events such as the dedication of a new building. Usually, the band leaders were the only professional musicians in the whole organization. This reminds one of the movie "The Music Man." Even then, the leader was not too professional. Band players often had to wear a very uncomfortable "buckskin" outfit. Imagine how they must have sweltered on a hot summer day! But, more often than not, they wore a comfortable attractive blue outfit with colorful brass buttons. They performed in band "shells" all over the state including on wildflower excursions. They sometimes raised money for charitable causes and, occasionally, donations were solicited. Their concerts were regular in the Colorado Springs area.

Life Along the Railroad Line in Basalt and the Frying Pan

Basalt

Basalt Gets its Name

Though squatters were in the area as early as 1880 and many Ute Indians before that, the first town in the Basalt area was begun in 1882. It was simply known as "Frying Pan." Henry Gannett, part of Doctor Hayden's Geological Survey, first named Frying Pan Creek. Later it was called the Frying Pan River. Gannett was the leader of the geographic and topographic phases of Hayden's survey. Mr. Gannett also named several other places in the area. This gives him the credit, also, for the first name of the town.

It is believed by some that the first name, Frying Pan, originated when some old-timer saw a skillet hanging from a tree. Someone had either been cooking delicious trout in it or using it to pan for gold. Miss Elizabeth Elliott, a former resident of Norrie and a school teacher in Glenwood, claims that some prospectors were about to make camp near Lake Ivanhoe when they noticed some Indians had camped there. They moved south toward Aspen in an attempt to escape them. Looking down below, they found Indians camped at the new site too. One of the prospectors reportedly exclaimed: "We have gone out of the Frying Pan and into the fire." Whatever the true story is, the name "Frying Pan" stuck.

When the few people in Frying Pan heard that a railroad was coming, the hamlet quickly moved to the north side of the river and became part of what was to become Aspen Junction. Dennis Barry moved his store and is said to have had the first post office in the history of Basalt in it. Red Duggan also moved his saloon. One account says that Basalt once had thirteen saloons; another account boasted of fifteen. These figures seem somewhat exaggerated, but there were enough saloons to make at least one prohibitionist lady complain to newspapers back in the Midwest. Western towns in those days had lots of saloons for sure. They were "men's towns" and the saloon was a place to gamble, socialize and drink. From the town's records of 1912 we read the following: "Minors, Indians, idiots, women and habitual drunkards are not allowed in the saloons."

A name change to "Basalt" became necessary when confusion arose in the postal system. Mail destined for Aspen Junction was being sent to Aspen and to Grand Junction. It was the railroad that requested the change. On nearby Black

Mountain were huge deposits of a porous black volcanic rock known as Basalt rock. This mineral in nature suggested a perfect name for the little town. Later, the mountain also experienced a name change to Basalt Mountain. Basalt was officially incorporated on August 26, 1901. A year later the U.S. Postal system also adopted the new name.

Early History

Prior to 1887, there were few stirrings to ever create a town site that would later be called Basalt.

Mr. Sopris, of Denver, for whom the beautiful mountain above Carbondale is named, was exploring in our area as early as 1860. He later became the mayor of Denver. The U.S. Government used the Meeker Massacre of 1879 as an excuse to run the Indians out of western Colorado. This paved the way for white settlers to safely move in. Things went slowly at first. Horses and mules were still the main modes of transportation. Wells Fargo wagons hadn't quite arrived yet, nor had Kit Carson's celebrated stage coaches. Many men walked great distances on foot carrying their knapsacks.

Basalt's first house, built by the Lucksingers. It still stands today.

The very first house in the valley was one constructed out of logs by Gabe and Julia Lucksinger. It had a sod roof and was an inn for travelers and for workers when it became too cold to stay in the flimsy tents. It is said that some type of old contract still exists that anyone buying the property, or any nearby, must make every effort to maintain that old house. Could it someday make a museum? To find the old house today a traveler should cross the new bridge in east Basalt and take the first left turn into a housing division on Riverside Drive. The old house is on the left and is unmistakable. It dates to the mid or late 1880s.

According to the excellent book by the Danielson brothers, whose father was an engineer on the Colorado Midland, Dennis Barry had a tent grocery store in little Frying Pan and Red Duggan had one of quite a few saloons. A man and woman were reportedly shot to death in one of the old saloons in Frying Pan. They were buried across the river near the current empty ranger station building (in the vicinity of the old George Smith home). It is believed the remains of those two were unearthed some years back when construction for a new home was taking place on the site. Others claim it was Indian remains dug up. Still others say it was old railroad workers who were buried there right on the spot where they were killed. Who knows for sure?

Many people at that time were staying in tents as they helped to build the charcoal ovens that still sit in what was once John Ruedi's property and, later, Emery Arbaney's ranch. The charcoal ovens supplied fuel for smelters in Aspen such as the Wheeler Smelter. Though Aspen had its own charcoal ovens and so did the Crystal Valley, apparently they weren't enough. Later, Sellar Meadow, above Nast, had fifteen ovens of its own. Wood makes charcoal. Coal makes coke. No coke ovens operated until large coal supplies were found near Carbondale and Glenwood. Workers would chop pine and piñon logs on the white hill above Basalt's Fairview Cemetery. Later, they also harvested pine from the red hills behind that. Wood was put into the back end of the ovens and came out the front as charcoal. The charcoal burned hotter and longer than regular wood. When coal came along, heating it in coke ovens produced "coke." It was much more efficient in train engines and caused minimal smoke.

Downtown Basalt and the Colorado Midland Railroad as it looked during the Midland's last days. The round house is presently part of Basalt Lions Park.

A Railroad Comes to Basalt

In the earliest of times, John Ruedi and some of the Lucksinger brothers came down from Aspen to settle. Ruedi settled in the area of Basalt South. It was as early as May 4, 1886, that Otmar Lucksinger first sold land to the Colorado Midland for construction of a railroad through town.

D.R.C. Brown came down from Aspen and began to plot the railroad tracks and a small town. The name of D.R.C. Brown has been famous in the Roaring Fork Valley for ages and still slips off the tongue of people today. In November of 1887 the railroad reached Aspen Junction (Basalt).

Basalt was not served by a railroad until silver was discovered in Aspen. It was incredible how fast a railroad could be thrown together in those days. Perhaps this is why the accidents were so frequent too! The D&RG, to digress just a little, went from Gilman in Eagle County to Glenwood in one six month summer-like period. The Midland went from Nast to Basalt in a year and a half. It was sometimes said that in good weather they could build a mile a day. Later, some railroads made five and seven and even ten miles a day.

The earliest rails were much less than ninety pounds (rails are measured by weight in terms of pounds per yard of length). It was found that even the ninety pound rails could not support the larger engines that came along and the heavier freight. At the outset the Midland did not even use metal tie plates or rail unions. The only anchoring they had was the rails to the wooden ties. If a storm came along and weakened the soil beneath, the engine tipped for sure, as did some of the cars. Accidents were especially bad on curves and near bridges.

Midland rails once lacked "union" plates like this one. Only wooden ties held the rails.

In books that list the number of buildings the railroad had in each little town on the Frying Pan, Basalt had, by far, the most. It was the "Who's Who" for a while on the western leg of the line. Eventually stops in Aspen and Glenwood outshined little Basalt. If the eastern slope was the "heart" of the Midland Railroad, then Basalt was the "liver." Basalt had a tool house, a bunk house, a section house, a cottage, a second cottage, a water tank, a coal house, an engine house with four of the largest helper engines, a sand house, a hand car house, a store house, an ice house, a pump house, a turntable 55, a roadmaster's office, a blacksmith shop, a coal trestle with 200 tons of coal, an oil house, a freight house, and a tool house, not to mention the depot and hotel.

The west end of the round house in Basalt. The three buildings above the engines are still in use.

See how important Basalt was? Contrast this with the Seven Castles stop that had only a "water closet." But these facilities were dwarfed by the ones in Leadville and Colorado Springs where many railroads competed for business. Basalt was a very important junction for the railroad. It was a blow to the ego of Basalt's residents when, later, the section house was moved to Cardiff. Perhaps the Midland felt it needed to keep a better eye on its chief rival, the D&RG with headquarters in Glenwood. Basalt's railroad water tank was huge. Great icicles hung from it in winter. At first the water came from the Frying Pan via a pump house. Later, when Basalt obtained a water system, the railroad hooked onto it too. The water tank sat right next to what became Silvy's Cabins later. Or, for new people in town, it sat right where a small half street leads south to the the swinging bridge. The Danielson brothers claim that they memorized every toot of their father's train whistle as it came into Basalt. It was kind of like a railroad Morse Code. They could tell the news of the day by the toots of the whistle.

By 1906, the dining cars were added to the trains. They were converted from passenger cars and still retained some seats on one end. Both the eating houses and the dining cars had their own silverware and china. Would-be collectors of today cherish the idea of having a set of these table items. The first china for the dining cars was called the Manitou pattern. It was made by the Onondaga Pottery Co. It was also used in the eating houses. The second pattern was called the Cascade made by John Maddock & Sons from England. Sugar bowls and creamers were made of real silver. Coincidentally enough, the names Manitou and Cascade were also the names of stops on the eastern side of the railroad line.

Railroad Disasters

Real disasters did happen right in Basalt. In Aspen Junction an accident happened which became known as the "Aspen Junction Horror." An engine was left parked too close to the main track. When the "laundry train" came by, a coach caught on the "laundry's" piston valve and broke it off. Steam and boiling water shot into the passing coach and killed most of the passengers in it. This happened on July 17, 1890.

A second terrible accident happened when the engineer parked the train between the big hotel eating house and the post office. The engineer and the fireman went into the drugstore to have a smoke. They had barely got inside when the engine exploded. Much of the boiler flew over the hotel and imbedded itself into the ground behind. A piece of pipe flew up to the next street and, reportedly, struck a girl. Others say that pieces of metal struck some of the buildings.

A train wreck near Seven Castles on May 14, 1914.

Another engine exploded in the early twentieth century. People standing nearby were scalded and cried out for help. About a dozen were scalded and another dozen injured. My mother once told me that people cried: "Oh, God, help me! Someone please help me!" Someone had let the water get too low in the boiler.

In 1904, they had such a heavy snowstorm in the Basalt area that it closed the railroad tracks. Aspen was marooned. (They rang the Maroon Bells for help. Tee hee!) Men came from Leadville to help and mother said prisoners were let out of Canon City to help remove the snow. She called it the winter of the big blockade. She said a few years after that the situation repeated itself more than once. It took ninety days in 1904 before fresh supplies reached Aspen and Basalt.

In another railroad accident in the vicinity of Basalt a man stuck his head out of the Midland to check on the weather and struck it on a bridge abutment. He died instantly. How fragile and precarious life was back then! It is still risky, we might add, today.

Early Residents

Other early landowners besides Lucksingers, Ruedi and D.R.C. Brown were: W. P. Bates, Michael McCaffery and Dan German. Lucksingers owned west and north Basalt and as far east as one of the alleys. Ruedi hugged the white hill area on the southeast where Emery Arbaney later bought. Soon these men started selling to homebuilders, businessmen and others. Emery Arbaney's son, Frederick (Bus) Arbaney, married a sweet and kind lady named Josephine. She survived her husband and still lives on the property today. Evidence of her kindness is that she donated the property on which the Basalt Middle School sits today. She is happy to report that the students have always treated her fairly and politely. When she and Bus remodeled their farm home years ago, they brought a small room over to the ranch that had once been attached to the Colorado Midland Depot in town. Still later remodeling revealed old Midland posters that had once hung in the depot still stuck to an interior wall of the addition.

Josephine tells a really good story about Emery Arbaney, her father-in-law. He bought his first new tractor after having used horses to pull the plows for decades. He let Bus and my brother, Fred, try it out first. They ran it over at least an acre of ground. Then Emery wanted a turn. He ran around a bit and then pulled it into the farmyard driveway. He started yelling "whoa! whoa!" as if it were a horse. It refused to stop and knocked out the water pump in the yard sending a spray skyward like Old Faithful. Then he crashed into the barn and brought it to a halt.

My brother, Fred Elmont, went to live with the Arbaneys at age eleven when my father, injured on a Frying Pan road crew, could no longer provide for his family adequately. Fred and Bus Arbaney became like brothers. Fred still has the first silver dollar Emery ever paid him in wages. As luck would have it, printed on the dollar is the year of Fred's birth. He has packed it around in a special plastic velvet-lined case. He kept it in a bank vault while he served his country as a paratrooper in WW II. Due to his efforts, the dollar is in absolute mint condition still today. He has promised it to his only daughter, Diane, someday.

One day Emery Arbaney assigned my brother to go divert some water out of the Roaring Fork river onto the family fields. Fred ("Tut") had no sooner opened the inlet when a highway patrolman stopped, thinking he had found a water thief for sure. To the trooper's great surprise, Tut went to his pickup and produced a document signed by none other than John Ruedi himself, giving Arbaneys perpetual rights to water out of both the Frying Pan and the Roaring Fork rivers. The trooper left just a little bit red-faced.

The Jonce Hough house in old Basalt.

My mother's relatives, the J.C. Houghs, were early residents of both the Ruedi area and, later, Basalt. They built the two-story yellow house with the seven gables that Bill Grange lives in today on the Aspen highway near the Basalt Store. "Jonce", as he liked to be called, lived at Ruedi as early as John Ruedi did. His wife, Chrissie, was the sister to our grandfather, Fred G. Jakeman, for whom Jakeman Creek near Thomasville is named. The Jakemans had come from Iowa long enough ago to be qualified as Colorado "natives." Fred G. married Lydia Hennings, also from Iowa, and they homesteaded on Jakeman Creek. My mother, Blanche Elmont, was their first child. Their home was taken apart after grandmother moved to Norrie when her husband died. It was re-assembled and is the second house on the right when entering Thomasville from Meredith.

My heart is attached to the Frying Pan—Basalt areas as I find my blood lines there. How exhilarating it was to discover a relative or two or more in every little hamlet on the Frying Pan. How wonderful it was to learn that a few of them were there as early as the famous John Ruedi. How nice it is to know that one of their homes still exists in

Jonce and Chrissie Hough.

Basalt and is still lived in by my friend Billy Grange. As Billy once told me recently that he had been offered big bucks for his property, I asked him why he didn't sell. To show how dedicated he is to the land and to his craft of farming he wanted to know what he could possibly do if he sold. I told him "....Travel the world, man!" He seemed the least bit interested. My good friend Reno Cerise has also been offered a goodly amount for his property nearby. He too has held out and is still farming, or at least his sons are. Reno! Sell! And we will visit Rome, Paris, Athens, London, Cairo, etc. I could fancy Reno saying "We've got to go home. It's time to milk the cows." "You're right!" chimed in Billy Grange. Some of my Basalt friends have been offered big money for their land. The usual response I get from them is: "What would I do if I sold?"

At Ruedi, when the train would bring the mail in 1887, John Ruedi would hand deliver it to Mrs. Hough. She would always thank him and promise him he could read her eastern magazines later. The Houghs lived on 220 acres north of John Ruedi in the vicinity where Fred McLaughlin later operated the Diamond G Guest Ranch. Today, part of the property is a campground with a portion of it (Little Maude Campground) named for my first cousin and her mother, Maude Usel of Fort Collins. Chrissie Hough felt lonely at Ruedi and felt her children should grow up near a good school and a church. So they moved to Basalt. There they had one of the finest orchards in town and Jonce raised potatoes and stored them in his own potato cellar. He loaded them onto the Colorado Midland and sold them as far away as Leadville.

Jonce felt the little white school at Emma was too far away for his children to walk in winter weather. It was one mile away. In warm weather they rode a horse. Jonce pressured the "powers that be" in Aspen and they soon built a nice brick two-story school in Basalt right on the county line. Gina Terliamis Cerise used to

The old school at Emma.

proudly tell me she went to that school. That is also the school where Bus Arbaney and his pal were once goofing around up in the attic. Bus was dropping spit wads down through a little hole in the ceiling onto the students below. Before anyone fully realized what was happening, Bus slipped and his big gangling legs broke through the plaster and into the classroom below. We don't know how he extricated himself from such an embarrassing situation, but we do know that Emery had to pay for the school repairs.

Disease struck the Hough family and much of Basalt at one time. Scarlet fever raged through the community. Two of the Hough daughters caught it but recovered. Little Chauncey, about seven, was not so lucky. He is buried in Basalt's Fairview Cemetery today and has a small white marble tombstone. Another brother after him survived to adulthood. For some reason the Houghs never got near the credit that John Ruedi got. They were in the area as early as he was and owned almost as much property. Perhaps "Ruedi" sounds better for a geographic location than "Hough." We will let it go, though it has sometimes tugged on the author's heart strings that his relatives didn't quite get their due."

Some of the early names in the Basalt-Woody Creek area were Arbaney, Cerise, Diemoz, Usel, Glassier, Grange, Arlian, Clavell, Hyrup and Vagneur. A very few of the Arbaneys worked for the Midland Railroad, but the rest of the immigrant families did not. They were mostly engaged in agriculture. We used to think Hyrups were Dutch but later learned they were Danish. Many of the other surnames came from Northern Italy from a little valley named Aosta. They had heard land was available in western Colorado and they came in droves. The climate and elevation were remarkably similar to what they had been used to at the foot of the famous Mont Blanc in Italy.

Aunt Linda Nelson of Blue Lake near El Jebel was an Arlian before she married Uncle Earl Nelson, the author's namesake and half-brother to the author's mother. Linda descended from these early Italian settlers. She recently toured northern Italy with her relatives and acted as translator for the beautiful little dialect spoken there, known as Patuá. It is part French and part Italian.

Water

My brother, Cliff Elmont, was a maintenance worker for the town of Basalt for thirty-three years. Among his duties was to care for the water supply. He says the old reservoir on the hill behind Albert Elmont's current rental home came down from Kelly Lake, still owned by the Emery Arbaney family. A big ditch fed part of the water to the Lucksinger Ranch and part to Basalt. People all over town obtained water from this big ditch before Basalt was able to afford its own nice system with covered pipes. The ditch used to freeze solid in the winter time. Arthur Bates solved the problem by taking his water out of a spring west of the old Gert Rhodes home, later owned by Alfred and Anna Sloss. That spring still produces water today. Bates sold water around town for 25¢ a barrel. It is strange that Basalt, which boasts of the best water in Colorado, would ever drink out of a dirt ditch. Cliff reports a funny little story that occurred when George Lucksinger was mayor of Basalt and JoAnne, his daughter, was town clerk. JoAnne was required to send water samples in to the state on a regular basis. One time she decided to boil the water first. A terse little note came back: "Quit boiling the water!" This happened in the 1950s when Walt Hyrup was the marshal in town.

Tombstones of Famous Basalt and Frying Pan People

1. NELSON / LUCILLE M. / JAMES A. / MOTHER / LYDIA ANN NEWKIRK / 1877 – 1969
2. DANIELSON
3. OTMAR LUCHSINGER
4. DAN GERMAN / 1843 – 1914 / ELIZEBETH GERMAN / 1849 – 1921
5. SLOSS
6.
7. LUCKSINGER / LUCHSINGER / MAYBIRD / AUG. 23, 1900 / JUNE 4, 1979 / JACOB / JAN. 22, 1898 / APR. 7, 1988
8. JAKEMAN / FRED G. / 1864 – 1902
9. CHAUNCEY HOUGH
10. ANNIE C. BLAIR / 1856 – 1936
11. LUCHSINGER / JULIA / 1847 – 1931 / GABRIEL / 1840 – 1926
12. HYRUP
13. BOGUE / PRUE T. / 1892 – 1981 / JESSE R. / 1888 – 1955
14. FRED A. SHEHI / 1864 – 1944
15. HOBERT WARREN LAMONT / OCT. 26, 1913 / OCT. 30, 1987
16. GEORGINA A. CERISE / JUNE 8, 1908 / AUG. 1, 1998
17. JOHN T. BUREMAN / APR. 27, 1865 / DEC. 31, 1952

1. Albert & Lucille Nelson. He helped Tucker McClure run "bulldozers" in Latin America. Lucille was Emery Arbaney's daughter. Lydia was Albert's mother.
2. A. L. Danielson, engineer on the Midland. Father of the two boys who wrote *Basalt, Colorado Midland Town.* A strict "prohibitionist."
3. Otmar Luchsinger. One of the original settlers of Basalt from Aspen . Sold land to the Midland and moved to current Cap K Ranch.
4. Dan German. One of Basalt's very earliest settlers. Moved to current ranch of the famous racecar driver, Wally Dallenbach.
5. Stirling P. Sloss. Father of Alfred and Alvin, twins. Built the beautiful two-story brick home still standing on Cap K Ranch. Sold out to Tucker McClure.
6. The Tierneys. Mrs. Ella Tierney built the first large brick store on Basalt's "Second Street." Later, the Sloss family owned it. Still later, it became the American Legion Hall. Today it is a business complex.
7. Notice the name change from Luchsinger to Lucksinger. Jake and Maybird were related to an original settler also named Jake Luchsinger. The younger Jake was once an Eagle County Commissioner.
8. The author's maternal grandfather. Homesteaded on Jakeman Creek. He and his wife, Lydia Ann Hennings, were both from Iowa. He was killed and Lydia married Nelson and, later, Newkirk.
9. Chauncey Hough. Killed in infancy by scarlet fever. Son of Jonce and Chrissie Hough who were instrumental in getting Basalt its first nice two-story brick school.
10. Beloved Annie Blair, wife of Frank Blair. Respectfully called "Mother Blair" by the railroad workers. Famous for her chicken dinners and homemade pies.
11. Gabe and Julia built an old log inn in Frying Pan Town. It still stands. It housed and fed stagecoach travelers and charcoal workers when it got too cold. It bordered John Ruedi's property.
12. Jens Peter Hyrup from Denmark. A Midland engineer once trapped in a snow storm for 45 days. His wife was from Germany. They had the first Christmas tree in all of Basalt. He was killed in a train accident near Cardiff. Father of all the later famous Hyrups.
13. Jesse Bogue. His home is in all the earlier photos of Basalt. It is now Java Joe's coffee house. Jesse was an engine repairman on the Midland Railroad. He and Prue have many descendants in the Basalt area.
14. Fred Shehi. Once lived at Seven Castles. Moved to Basalt. Was a confirmed bachelor. Townspeople cleaned house for him and brought food.
15. Hobert LaMont. He and his wife's relatives go back a long way in the Norrie area. Betty and David still own property up there today.
16. Gina Terliamis Cerise. Famous sheep raiser. Born a Cerise, married a Terliamis. After he died she married her deceased sister's husband and became a Cerise again. Walked her sheep all the way from Basalt to Lake Ivanhoe.
17. John T. Bureman, an old railroad engineer and father of the famous "Swede" Bureman, garage owner in the old Midland Railroad Depot. The author was a housekeeper for John as a teenage boy. Swede paid him.

The Colorado Midland pumped its water for its large wooden tank on Main Street from the Frying Pan River. The busiest street in town back then was probably the County Line Road which we kids always called Second Street. The downtown street was too crowded by the railroad lines. A Glenwood firm got the contract for installing Basalt's first real water system at a cost of $11,000. The Danielson brothers refer to this engineering feat on page 20 of their book *Basalt, Colorado Midland Town.* Water rent, after the new pipes went in, was listed at $4 per quarter.

As a kid I remember that the water from the drinking fountain on Main Street (now Midland Avenue) was cold and delicious. It came out of a wonderful spring at the foot of Basalt Mountain at about 58 degrees temperature. We never heard of putting chlorine in it in the old days. Yuck! The fountain existed between the Two Rivers Café and the building just east of it. One day a big dog raised up on his hind legs and started drinking from the fountain. Though I admired his resourcefulness, I hesitated to drink from the same fountain for some time afterward. As soon as the new water system was in, the Midland Railroad promptly hooked onto it.

Early Basalt, showing where the wye for the railroad used to be. Now Basalt Lions Park, the library and municipal buildings occupy the middle of the wye.

High Line Road

All the time Frying Pan town existed, and later Aspen Junction and Basalt, there was no official Frying Pan wagon road. Before the railroad, supplies had come in by mule train and wagon. Now a wagon road up the Frying Pan was sorely needed. In 1899 the state legislature set aside the sum of $7,000 for such a road. The road was supposed to go from Basalt to Ruedi. It was finally completed in 1905. It was called the High Line and was well-named. It wound like some crooked string high up on the hill. My mother and her family often used it or took the train from Norrie to Ruedi and, thence, to Basalt by wagon. The road was a 'beast" in winter and was often impassable. I have heard old tales about placing a hot rock or a brick under a quilt with the feet perched on the rock to keep warm. This is how they traveled with just a horse and wagon in cold weather. The road was created by teams of horses pulling scrapers. How I would have loved to re-live just one day back then for a ride on the High Line in a wagon or buggy and a trip on the train through the Busk-Ivanhoe Tunnel. But another person said: "The only good thing about the good old days is that they are gone!" I guess it all depends on one's perspective. As the High Line became bogged down with thick red mud, how grateful the travelers must have been for the train. There was still considerable risk in a journey by train. Amtrak still takes a tumble occasionally today.

The old county line horse and buggy road above Cap K Ranch. Just a few miles upstream, the road switched to the south side of the river and ran to Ruedi.

Mr. Joe Gregg, Jr., part-owner of the Cap K Ranch today, and owner of the old Tucker McClure home, said the old High Line road had very clever culverts made of red sandstone. When runoff was sparse, the water simply seeped its way through red rock culverts beneath the road. Where "gullywashers" were known to come down, the culverts were actually arched with a keystone holding the others in place. Rarely did the road wash out thanks to these cleverly built culverts. The floods might build up a layer of dirt on top of the road requiring a simple grader to come by. Seldom did the whole culvert have to be rebuilt. Our ancestors were no dummies, were they?

Basalt Businesses

While Basalt was still called Aspen Junction, the first newspaper in town was the *Eagle County Examiner*. It published from 1894–1896. Next followed the *Basalt Tribune* from 1896–1898. The *Basalt Journal* followed next from 1897–1910. The heavy winter of 1899 caused the *Basalt Journal* to run short on paper and, also, coal and supplies. Starting in 1909 the *Basalt Eagle* published the news until 1912. Then Basalt experienced a lapse in journalism. The *Frying Pan* published from 1922–1924, just after the demise of the Midland.

Basalt's first train depot was bigger and fancier than the current one which has been restored to its grandeur. It was longer and contained an eating house. It had a split level roof, different from the current one. Basalt's hotel was the very first eating house on the Frying Pan leg of the Midland. When the new eating house opened, no more meals were ever served in any depots. When dining cars arrived in the first part of the twentieth century, eating houses, as such, were no longer needed. The hotel and eating house has experienced different names. It was the Frontier Lodge when the author was young. Today it is the Primavera. At one time in its history, according to my mother, it also housed a CCC Camp. Mother helped with the laundry for a while and helped a lady in distress when she accidentally splashed bleach in her eyes. Mother flushed them repeatedly with cold water and saved the lady's sight. The original depot burned in a massive fire. It was 35 feet wide by 70 feet long. Its replacement, still existing, was (and is) 20 ft. by 60 ft. The newer depot had to experience some changes in order to become Swede's Standard Garage. It underwent further changes when Mr. Whitney McClelland began to restore it with the help of his father in 1969. It currently houses the Alpine Bank.

Early Basalt businesses were: Basil Smith and Co.; Tierney Co. (general mercantile); Zimmerman Drug; W. W. Frey, grocer; Matt Hanson, boots and shoes; E. B. Kelly, saloon; Epperson, saloon; railroad hotel and inn; a boarding house west of Smith's (formerly Gould's Hotel); post office (first one ever in Smith's Store); Zimmerman (also a notary public, an agent for Johnson Undertakers in Aspen, a real estate agent); M. B. Louthou, postmaster 1890; Arthur J.

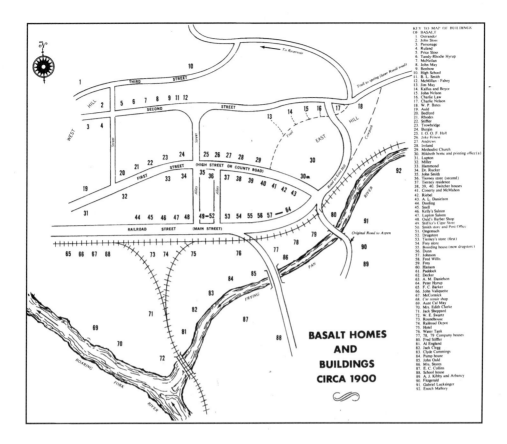

**BASALT HOMES
AND
BUILDINGS
CIRCA 1900**

Kibby, next postmaster; Basil Smith, postmaster again; J. P. Jones, Justice of the Peace; Frank Hotchkiss, constable; M. McNeilan, doctor; P. T. Rucker, doctor; W. G. Fleming, railroad agent; Grant Ruland, school principal; and Colonel Stiffler, auctioneer.

At one time, according to pioneers Edna Sweet and Anna Olson, Basalt's population reached 1,500 souls. I wonder if that doesn't rival the population of today. The first telegraph was constructed by Henry Gillespie. There is a Gillespie Street in Aspen and one in El Jebel. The same Gillespie built the mansion in El Jebel that Bonnie Williams lives in now. Amy Favre once had it as part of his farm. Methodist, Episcopal, Catholic and Presbyterian churches all moved into Basalt rather early (1905 and thereabouts.) This helped counteract the many saloons with a good dose of temperance. There were a few murders in Basalt in its early days. That was unlike the forties, fifties and sixties when the author reports that there were none.

W. W. Frey must have had something to do with freight and passenger shipments on the Midland Train. When Jim Crowley bought the building, he found old ledgers listing passengers and freight shipped and costs. It even had gas pumps outside in all the older photos. Uncle Earl Nelson reopened the old

Frey Store in the 1950s when he opened Basalt's first Co-op. He sold off much of the old merchandise he found in the back rooms. Talk about a "journey back in time," or "a walk down memory lane." I was fascinated by old tablets, pencils, metal hardware products, etc. Even the old interior of the building was fascinating. It reminded me of the old J. C. Penney building in Glenwood during the forties. When a sale was made, the clerk put the money in a little suspended metal cup with the sales slip clipped to the bottom. Then she pulled a wooden handle attached to a rope and the money "zinged" its way upstairs where the cash register was. A clerk up there made the proper change and zinged it back down to the ground floor. Except the Frey store did not "zing" its money upstairs. It did everything on the ground floor. It seems like I saw this same system in the old Frey Store but I never saw anyone use it. Perhaps they "had their wires crossed."

The sidewalk in front of the old Frey Store will forever hold bad memories for me. When I was a two year old, a large vicious German Shepherd dog attacked me out front even though my mother had me by the hand. It tore my left ear half loose from my face. Old Pop Waite had studied to be a doctor but did not pass the final exams. So he became a pharmacist instead and ran the drug store next door. He still remembered how to stitch people up and mother knew it. She rushed me in. I don't remember the stitching but I remember the dog attack as if it were yesterday. I still have a little white scar up along the ear to remind me of those days. Bill Eppley reports that the same old dog was the

Teenagers gather in old Basalt.

meanest one in town. I think it belonged to the Freys and was probably protecting their property in its mind. One day Bill Eppley was parked in front of the drugstore with his little niece. The dog made a "beeline" for the niece when Eppley commanded his own dog, King, to "get him." Bill reports that his dog killed that vicious old thing and solved the problem forever. It seems that the more traumatic the story, the more we remember it.

The drugstore had earlier been a boarding house. It had a cute little grassy park due east of it. Pop Waite was a son of the governor of Colorado. His wife was a sister to Mrs. Alex Arbaney, Jr. Waite had some lovely daughters and my handsome brother, Fred, used to "romance them." When Waite moved to Grand Junction, he purchased a movie theatre. That is the last we heard of him.

Basalt Ranger Station

The Basalt Ranger Station served us well in the twentieth century. The first ranger that the Carbondale office has records of was James R. Ahl. He was over the Frying Pan District from 1928–1929. Next came Percy Ray for a longer stint in office, from 1929–1941. From 1941 to 1945 was our old friend, Thomas C. Pender. I had a crush on his daughter, Mary Caroline. She still frequents the Frying Pan area in summer. From 1945–1954, Mr. Pender served in the Eagle Ranger District. From 1954–1956, another old friend, Paul Reedy, was the ranger. The sturdy building may have sat vacant after Mr. Reedy, or else was shared by personnel from the Carbondale District. Though cars have been seen parked there, the building looks largely unused today, at least for ranger purposes. This information was courteously and helpfully provided by Ms. Cathy Carlisle of the Sopris District, White River National Forest, Carbondale, Colorado. What a genial hostess she is!

The old ranger station sits on the left side of the road approximately one-half mile east of the barber shop in Basalt. Some other modern day residents in the vicinity of the ranger station are: my old high school buddy, Darol Woolley (the most helpful person imaginable toward the publication of this book). Near him are the Michael Bairs and their parents, Pete and Gingie Bair. Mr. Joaquin Blaya lives farther east on the bend in the road. His house is one that I covet most of all on the entire Frying Pan road. Formerly living

Looking east on Basalt's 3rd Street (Sopris Dr). March 1948.

in that vicinity were the James Maddalones, the Frank Pecjaks, the Dale Grants and the Johnny Hyrups. The Grants are now both deceased and the Johnny Hyrups live on a lovely ranch in Parachute, Colorado. Mention the name Hyrup and you conjure up old memories for sure of the Colorado Midland Railroad.

It is regretful to the author not to be able to mention all the residents of any given locality. But this is virtually impossible unless people send me some data of their own like Mrs. Lynn Nichols from Cap K Ranch did. Some people were, and are, so prominent that they automatically beg inclusion in this book. For example: In a small house west of Mr. Blaya lived Tiny Smith. She was a daughter of the prominent early Basalt merchant, Mr. W. W. Frey. He was the only Basalt merchant, of those early ones, to still be in business after the turn of the century. His building has been used for various enterprises and still stands. The old business ledgers from his store were found when Mr. Jim Crowley operated the Midland Bar and Café there. Said ledgers are in Mr. Crowley's possession.

Basalt Memories

If the reader feels Basalt is getting slighted in any way in this book, he is referred to the author's earlier book, *Basalt, Friendly Town*, available in the Basalt Regional Library. It covers Basalt in great detail street by street and house by house. It covers mainly the period from 1945–1965, when a lot of the old railroaders were still alive.

John Bureman was one of those railroaders. He was the father of the illustrious and celebrated Swede (Eric) Bureman. He lived on Swede's property near the river by the old Pueblo Bridge. He had his own little house. I used to cook and clean house for him and stoke the fires when I was a teenager. Swede promptly paid me every week. John's idea of a good breakfast was a waffle made from scratch and an egg cooked in two inches of bacon grease. He would have me drop the egg in when the grease was hot and wait until it floated to the surface. He would "lick his chops" as I placed it on the plate next to the waffle. It's an absolute miracle that he lived into his mid nineties from what he ate. There were two jobs that I told Swede I would not do: clean out the chemical "porta-potty" and dump the Copenhagen spit bucket. Swede got old Dave Olson to do that. It did not escape my attention that as Dave was dumping a month's accumulation of "snuff" into the Frying Pan, Ikey (Floyd) May was a block down the river getting his morning bucket of water. Yuck!

Often old John would fall out of bed in the middle of the night and could not get up 'til I arrived in the mornings to check the fire. He was normally just fine down there on the floor because the room was cozy warm. One day, while finding him on the floor, I asked what happened to his toenail on his big toe. He told me he was on the back end of a huge railroad tie when the man on the front stumbled. This jerked the tie out of both their hands and it landed right on John Bureman's toe. The nail was at least four times thicker than it should have been. Though some may doubt me, I actually had to trim it with the hedge clippers provided by Swede and a large file. Now there is a true railroad "mini-story."

Three Basalt boys on the ice in about 1945.

On the first sharp curve beyond Johnny Hyrup's property, Larry Terrell and I almost killed the mailman, Grandpa Newkirk. We were up above on the old Carl Adams' ranch road. We decided to roll a huge rock down into the Frying Pan River. We no sooner got it rolling well when we noticed "Newkie" coming around the bend in his mail truck with his faithful dog, King. We shuddered with fear. We had never killed anything bigger than a rabbit. A time or two we closed our eyes afraid to look. We imagine that Newkie said something to his dog as he undoubtedly heard the "swoosh" of the rock half the size of his truck speeding just two yards behind him as it crashed with a thunderous splash into the river. "You hear anything, King?" We hope he never saw anything either! That cured us royally. We never rolled another rock again. The experience for my brother, Tut, must have been dèjá vu. Years earlier he and Bus Arbaney did the same thing with a much larger rock. It took them two or three days, off and on, to loosen it enough to roll. It did not narrowly miss anyone down below, but undoubtedly gave them the same "rush" or thrill, that is, until we noticed grandpa coming. He was the third husband to grandma, after Jakeman and Nelson. How many people have to risk total oblivion before foolish youth finally learn?

Just a little ways above that first sharp curve I had my first run-in with an owl. It was the same year as the rock rolling. I saw a little owl in an oak tree to the left of the road. I was sure it was a tiny little orphan. I attempted to rescue it and give it a good home. It nearly clawed me alive. I have not had such a rush of adrenalin since. I came to find out it was a full-grown Pygmy Owl! Where was Mr. Audubon when I needed him?

On that same first sharp curve the saddest thing that ever happened to us and our favorite summer tourists occurred. Year after year the Jess Horners from Blytheville, Arkansas, and the Fred Fleemans from Texas were perpetual summer residents of Charlie Bowers' rental cabins. Charlie was the owner of the Basalt Sundry. The Jess Horner family were dealers in General Motors cars. We always anticipated their arrival to see what the latest model of Oldsmobile or Cadillac was. One summer day their eldest of two daughters, "Jimmy", was driving her jeep up the Frying Pan with a good friend, Linda Taylor. They always came with a guest each summer. Jimmy read a "love letter" from home as she drove. Her Jeep hit some corduroys in the road and bounced them right into the river. There was no guard rail then. They both managed to get out of the Jeep and cling to its roof. It was high water season in July. As they clung there they yelled for help. A passing fisherman made a poor split-second decision. He swam out to the Jeep and attempted to rescue both girls at once. As he headed for shore Jimmy, the heavier of the two, slipped out of his grasp and down the river. Linda and the fisherman made it to shore safely.

Two months went by with no word of Jimmy's body. It was the most unfortunate luck for my Uncle Earl Nelson to be the one who found her body near the Hook's Bridge in the newer part of Basalt, which has just recently been annexed. He said he had trouble sleeping for months after the discovery. This had such a terrible effect on Jess Horner and his wife, Lorna, and their other daughter, June, that their visits to Basalt became less and less. One summer, much later, we had the privilege of going on a picnic to the Snowmass area with Lorna. After that we never heard from her again. Via the grapevine we learned that Jess had gone out of his mind with grief over the incident and chose to live in the servant's quarters behind his own home. How saddened we all were. For a few more summers, the Fleemans continued to come. Then Charlie Bowers sold out and moved to Apache Junction, Arizona. We never saw the Fleemans again. It was with the greatest surprise that I later learned that Fierman Arbaney and Horace Hendricks were silent partners in the business with Charlie.

Frying Pan River Fishing and Terrific Tourists:

The Frying Pan River may well be the foremost fly fishing stream in all of America. In the summer of 2002 I counted twelve fishermen in one spot. In other areas I counted six and eight and so on. Below the Ruedi Dam they were thick in clusters as they tried their luck by the spillway. I saw ladies fishing with their husbands and deemed them very smart. It's better to tag along with hubby than to become a fisherman's widow. Better yet, learn the sport and join him! One couple sat lovingly together on the same rock in midstream fishing in opposite directions.

In one area, I saw an entire family fishing together. The very youngest sat on a rock merely watching, but having fun nonetheless. I asked a man from Kansas which fly was having the most luck. He said: "A Blue Wing. It is a cousin to a Mayfly."

Fishermen ply the waters of the spillways at Ruedi Dam.

Seeing these fishermen, even in wintertime, brought back pleasant memories of the days when I was a teenager working in Charlie Bowers' Basalt Sundry. Charlie was quite a fisherman himself and often left work to take his favorite summer tourists to some red hot fishing hole. Charlie came to Basalt in the forties with his good friend, Walt Matthews, who settled in Aspen and opened a full-fledged drugstore there. Charlie's was only a sundry because he had no pharmacist. A sundry offered varied and multiple supplies—everything from angle worms at fifty cents a carton, to over-the-counter medicines, gifts, liquors and ice cream. We had one of the best soda fountains in western Colorado.

A customer could still buy a few out-dated items from the days of old Pop Waite, who was a druggist. One of the old items had a real value to garage owner Swede Bureman. Swede had been having trouble with a wino or two leaving liquor bottles around his business and annoying lady customers in the process. Rejecting all of Charlie's suggestions for modern laxatives, Swede proceeded to the back room where the old stuff was. There he spied an ancient box of Grandma Sill's Herbal Innerclean. "That's it!" shouted Swede. "But," protested Charlie, "you might kill him." "I hope he _ _ _ _s all over the place!" interjected Swede. As Swede exited the store he proceeded to pour the entire contents of the box into the wine bottle, shaking the contents of the quart-sized bottle as he went. Later, we heard that the wino didn't show up for several days.

(Seemed to have been confined to his home for some reason.)

It was that same wonderful Swede, extremely generous to young kids, who tried to stop the same winos from urinating on the front of his garage in broad daylight. The winos never seemed to notice, or care, that high-class ladies were having their cars filled with gas nearby. Swede rigged up multiple layers of electrical wires across the front of the garage and hooked them to a 12-volt battery. My brother, Cliff, and I were present when the first wino decided to relieve himself. Like a bolt of lightning on a cloudy day, we heard a loud crackling sound as a sharp blue flame shot up into the victim's body. We had never seen anyone take off so fast, not even at a track meet, as he struggled to zip his pants in a semi-stupor and then proceeded to set a new world record for the hundred-yard dash. The wires solved the problem just as Grandma Sill took care of the bottle problem. As an added bonus, the same day, we got to watch Darien's cute little dog, Corky, take off like a rocket when he tested those same wires. Cliff says he was moving so fast he rolled the last two yards home to his own porch.

Three of the most famous men who ever lived in Basalt, Bill Lucksinger, Ben Darien, and Swede Bureman standing in front of Swede's Garage, now Alpine Bank. 1943.

Well, back to Charlie's sundry. Among the dry flies I liked to sell were Mosquitoes, Gray Hackle Yellows and Wooly Worms. I loved to pretend I was the world's living expert on dry flies. Whenever someone came along that really knew his business about flies, I suddenly changed the subject. Charlie, and his wife, LaVina, were true fishing experts. In Charlie's day people used a lot of live bait in early summer when the waters were still a little muddy. Halgremites were a perennial favorite. Each July they magically turned into willow flies, another favorite. Those lucky enough to catch some, fished with them. Today, I am told they are all gone. Fortunately, there is no whirling disease in our waters. In 2001, I saw a large crew of Game and Fish Dept. people out in the middle of the Frying Pan checking for the disease. They found none. Some claim it is in ponds and still water where the malady seems to thrive.

We had two of the world's best game wardens in our Basalt area. Mr. Chub Downey was one and Mr. Bob Terrell was the other. Mr. Terrell had an uncanny knack for catching a poacher or a fisher without a license. He seemed to be able to "smell one out." Often the confiscated game was donated to a worthy cause. If rumor was correct, the chili con carne at our high school was made out of captured illicit venison. The head cook at school was Mr. Downey's wife, Carrie.

Basalt Post Office

Basalt sits at about 6,625 feet above sea level. Until modern times it has remained largely a small community. In about 1895 it experienced quite a building boom including twenty-five new structures and a new Methodist Church. In 1905 it looked rather prosperous. Today it has benefited from the prosperous ski haven nearby known as Aspen. It serves as a bedroom community for that resort. Many hundreds live in Basalt today as its buildings occupy the hills to the north and an entire new community to the south. Midland Avenue, the old Main Street, boasts many new buildings and businesses. Across the river, toward old Emma, more signs are evident of a prosperous town, and the place even boasts of a beautiful new post office and a roundabout. What a symbol of pride and prosperity the new post office is as it sits on property near the former Joe Fiou farm!

The post office I remember first was run by a Mrs. Paddock. She lived in the home west of the Catholic Church which is now a rectory. Of course, my Aunt Maude Elmont, who lived to be one hundred and one years old, ran the best post office ever for twenty-six years. She served in at least five different buildings. In one, a gas leak blew the roof off and settled it down one foot crooked while she was out for lunch. Angels must have been looking out for her. Once, as a little boy, I had to squeeze through the stamp window to let Aunt Maude into her second post office by the eastern alley. She had locked herself out. Years later in that same post office, as I helped her stamp the voluminous Christmas mail, an old drunk sauntered in through the east alley door. Never

Cliff Elmont, formerly of Meredith, poses with his Aunt Maude Elmont, postmaster in Basalt for twenty-six years. At her death at age 101, Maude was the oldest living resident of the Basalt–Frying Pan area.

had I seen Aunt Maude rise up in such majesty, frail as she was, and order that old drunk out in no uncertain terms. "Yes, ma'am!" he obediently replied.

Maude made dozens of close friends in that job and they wrote to her for years and visited occasionally in summertime. She became a celebrity in her advanced age as she reached a milestone of being the oldest surviving resident of the Basalt–Frying Pan area. The city of Carbondale, where she then lived, put on a celebration for her 101st birthday and the mayor came. I will not forget taking her to Norrie where she once lived. It was 1995. She was astonished at the amount of green growth on the hillsides. It is no wonder she felt the place was so bare in the early 1900s. The largest lumber operation on the entire western slope had taken down most of the trees. The lumber harvesters, non-existent today, had contributed almost single-handedly to that "lunar-looking landscape."

Basalt To Ruedi

Wooden Handle and Wally Dallenbach

What a clever name for a Frying Pan resort! Years ago it actually had a twenty-foot-long handle over the driveway attached to a large metal frying pan. Originally it was the home of one of the earliest settlers, Dan German. It was later the old Grub place. Later Phil Smith, who maintained the road, lived there. The pavement used to stop right there on the bend in the road just above the Wooden Handle. It had been called the Wooden Handle ever since the early forties. Later it was owned by a gentleman from Aspen. His name was Army Armstrong. He also owned the Copper Kettle in Aspen.

The current owner is a famous race car driver named Wally Dallenbach. He first visited our area in 1973 on a motorcycle with his wife Peppy on the back. He had just come from a big racing win in California. His children grew up here in Basalt. They are Wally Jr., Colleen and Paul. They went to Basalt schools and my Aunt Linda taught two of them. She proudly recalls that. Like many, Wally became enchanted with the picturesque little valley. As soon as the scenic property went on the market, he bought it.

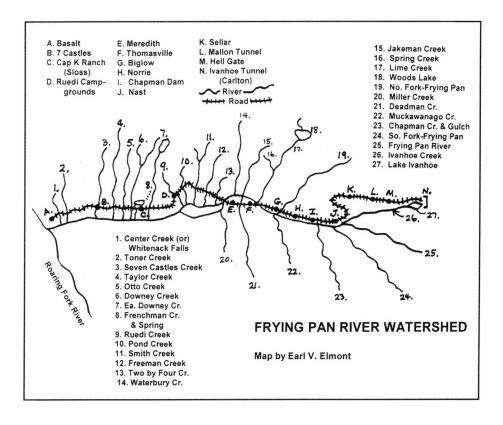

A. Basalt
B. 7 Castles
C. Cap K Ranch (Sloss)
D. Ruedi Camp-grounds
E. Meredith
F. Thomasville
G. Biglow
H. Norrie
I. Chapman Dam
J. Nast
K. Sellar
L. Mallon Tunnel
M. Hell Gate
N. Ivanhoe Tunnel (Carlton)

15. Jakeman Creek
16. Spring Creek
17. Lime Creek
18. Woods Lake
19. No. Fork-Frying Pan
20. Miller Creek
21. Deadman Cr.
22. Muckawanago Cr.
23. Chapman Cr. & Gulch
24. So. Fork-Frying Pan
25. Frying Pan River
26. Ivanhoe Creek
27. Lake Ivanhoe

1. Center Creek (or) Whitenack Falls
2. Toner Creek
3. Seven Castles Creek
4. Taylor Creek
5. Otto Creek
6. Downey Creek
7. Ea. Downey Cr.
8. Frenchman Cr. & Spring
9. Ruedi Creek
10. Pond Creek
11. Smith Creek
12. Freeman Creek
13. Two by Four Cr.
14. Waterbury Cr.

FRYING PAN RIVER WATERSHED

Map by Earl V. Elmont

Wally started drag racing at age fifteen. Eventually he was into the big time in such races as the Indy 500. All in all, he drove five championship cars for that big event. His brother Bob is a minister for a Denver church. Wally too is a devout Christian. He once lived with his brother in Denver. When he got married, he honeymooned with his brand new wife in the Frying Pan area. He is approximately sixty-five years old and has maintained a residence at his current place for eleven years. He is often gone on business and other pursuits, but he spends all the time he can at his Frying Pan home.

Bob Larson looks after the place when Wally is gone. He is a long-time Basalt resident who is liked by all who know him. Bob explains that the cabins on the property are for long-term occupation and not just a day or two or a weekend. To manage the place properly, Bob lives right there in one of the cabins. He and Wally seem to hit it off well at the old Wooden Handle.

An old wagon at Dallenbach's place.

Many sporting events are held on the property. Motorcycle rallies have taken place there. The property has been seen bedecked with flags and banners with all sorts of motor homes and other vehicles parked there. Kayaks have even been seen floating in the river to the south. It may be the busiest little spot on the Frying Pan today. Locals seem proud to mention that a famous race car driver has chosen to live among them. We got a photo of him posed with his wife by the old homestead Dan German made. It still stands with its distinctive markings on the logs from old Dan German's axe.

Wally competed in 180 Indy Car Races. That almost boggles the human mind. In addition, he won the Milwaukee 200, the California 100 twice, the California 500 and the Trenton 200. His best year was in 1973. How interesting that it should be the same year he found the Frying Pan.

At age 15 he was too young to race so he became an owner and mechanic of a stock car. At age 17 he was now legal and became interested in drag racing. He accomplished 80-some wins in five years. At 21 years of age he qualified for oval racing and, in the next four years, he won his fair share of races. He was a close friend to Mario Andretti and other famous racers.

All of his children have been involved in one way or another in racing. The two boys actually drove racing cars like their father. Peppy became Director of Registration for the Indy 500. Wally Jr's. wife Robin races too. By age 14 she had racked up 200 wins in midget car racing. In 1979 she won the National

Wallly Dallenbach in 1968 at the Indianapolis Motor Speedway.

Championship in AA Midget Car Racing. She was a pace car driver at the Indy 500. Daughter Colleen is currently Office Manager for Pac West Racing Teams.

Wally Sr. has had various sponsors including Sprite soda and STP additive. He beat Mario Andretti once by five seconds. Wally has packed a lucky 1922 silver dollar in his pocket since 1970. That dollar traveled over 6,435 miles with him in various races. In 1972, in the Indy 500, his car caught fire three times. He stayed in the race, though a little singed.

Annette (Peppy) Dallenbach has followed him since they were first married in 1960. She was with him at the Indy 500 for his first race on that track on Memorial Day in 1967. He was considered a "rookie" then, but is no rookie now. He is one of the most famous men on the Frying Pan and joins the ranks of other celebrities who once, or are now, settled there such as Ringo Starr, Neil Diamond and John Denver.

When Wally quit racing he became Director of Competition for the Indy 500. He held that job until 1979. He was also Chief Steward for the same course and held that job until 1999. He was Chief Steward for CART (Championship Auto Racing Teams). In that capacity he had a lot of power. He wore a cowboy hat and at least one driver referred to him as "sheriff." If someone was intentionally reckless in one race or a qualifying race, Wally had the power to bar him from a future race. He and his children became champions of "safety first." Wally designed race courses as early as 1982. Many said it would be extremely difficult to replace him as Chief Steward. He said he would "....hang around thru 2000 to help the new guy."

He and Peppy have added some wonderful additions onto their home on the Frying Pan. Peppy is the best decoration in the whole house. I am sure Wally would agree as he sits there "whiffing" some of her culinary delights. Fame and fortune has not tainted the couple. They are just as warm and amiable and humble as anyone the author has ever met.

Twice a year they sponsor, from their little grassy paradise, a motorcycle rally for charity. It is called the Colorado 500 Charity Motorcycle Ride. People pay a fee to sign up. The ride runs to Aspen and over to Crested Butte, from thence to Ouray, Colorado, then back to Crested Butte and Aspen, finishing at Snowmass. The last time the charity ride was sponsored, 300 bikers showed up. So now you know what all that activity is about each time you drive past. Wally and his associates have raised the astounding sum of $800,000 dollars for charity. Much of it goes here locally to Western Colorado. We take our hats off to you Wally, Peppy and family. No one was ever more welcome in the Frying Pan Valley, not even John Ruedi himself.

Wally Dallenbach's comfortable log home two miles from Basalt.

Toner Creek

Just west of Otto Hyrup's place was Toner Creek. Though John Smith never built a home there, he and his sons raised horses on the property. They leased pasture and raised Belgians and Perscherons. The Smiths sold to the Game and Fish Department which did build a house there and maintained a ranch. There were several small beaver ponds above the house on Toner Creek. They were stocked with edible-sized trout. Mr. Bob Terrell, one of the two local game wardens (Chub Downey was the other), would take his wife Ellen and children Larry and Dale to the ranch to fish. They would invite me to come along. We males did the fishing and Mrs. Terrell did the cleaning and cooking. She rolled the fish in corn meal and fried them right there on the bank. I remember that they were most delicious.

On that same ranch, in later years, Larry Terrell would hunt for magpies. They had become too numerous and were pestiferous in the area. The government offered a bounty of 25¢ per egg or 25¢ per pair of legs. Larry outdid himself in earning money by this endeavor. I hated to see the magpies killed. They always seemed like such a beautiful majestic bird. They let out a distinctive "scolding" sound and can, indeed, be a nuisance at times. They will raid another bird's nest and eat the offspring. Like gulls, they seem omnivorous.

Castle View and the Famous Hyrups

Larry Hyrup was the only child of Otto and Faye Hyrup and lived with his very pretty wife Johnnie on a ranch at Castle View. Larry also owned a sawmill. The children were Larry Ray, Mara Lynn, Allen Lee, Jon Wayne and Jimmy. Pat Hyrup Yale, a relative of theirs from Buena Vista, Colorado, believes Jon Wayne is the one who still lives on the property. It is said that when part of the land was sold to Phil Sterker of Texas the contract stipulated that as long as any Hyrup was left alive, he got to live in that place. Larry Hyrup's parents also lived at Seven Castles (or Castle View) up the road. Faye was a sister to Carrie Downey and Nettie Fuhriman.

Larry used to truck some of his lumber over to Denver and other parts. It is said that Kendall Sloan bought a big Ford truck with an extra long bed to help Larry ship his logs around the Frying Pan area. Larry was accidentally killed on Loveland Pass around 1958 or 1959 in a tragic accident involving his big truck. Johnnie lives with her new husband, Jack Jackson, in the old Chub and Carrie Downey home in Basalt. Apparently they have done a nice job in remodeling that older home. The author hopes there will always be a Hyrup at Castle View. We have fond memories of long tall Larry and his most attractive wife.

Phil Sterker bought the land east of Larry Hyrup and built a lodge. There is a small pond out front full of cattails. Bill Eppley, formerly of Basalt, says that he built that pond. Recently extensive work has been done to upgrade the pond.

East of the pond is an assortment of cabins, trailers and homes.

The earliest Hyrup in the whole area was Jens Peter Hyrup from Denmark. Jens Peter Hyrup was an engineer on a train trapped in a snowstorm on a different occasion in a year other than 1899. He was snowbound also around Hagerman for approximately 45 days. Enough food arrived in emergency manner to spare his life. One of Larry Hyrup's sons made a trip to Denmark not too many years ago. About twenty miles outside of Copenhagen he found a whole town named Hyrup. The original Hyrup farmhouse is still standing in Denmark. Due to various wars the property was once in Denmark but is now in Germany. At least one of the Hyrups, on the maternal side, came from Germany. Her name was Anna Murman and she was Jens Peter's wife. Her relatives always sent her Christmas ornaments from Germany and the Hyrups were said to have had the very first Christmas tree in all of Basalt. How is that for exciting trivia?

Jens Peter Hyrup brought his wife Anna and two children to Basalt in the early 1890s. The children were Christian and Eugenia. They came here from Helena, Montana. We always thought they were Dutch. Patricia Yale Hyrup thinks the fact that one of her brothers was called "Dutch" is where the legend began. When Jens Peter first moved to Basalt he lived in a house on the corner where old Main Street met Second Street (near the current barber shop). Later, Walter Hyrup lived there until the house burned down and he had to build a new one.

Jens Peter had other sons besides Chris and the one daughter Eugenia. Otto, Walter and Alfred Hyrup were all born in that house on the corner. I assume his very attractive granddaughter Eugenia is named for that great aunt. Johnny Hyrup is a brother to Eugenia. There were other daughters too in Walter's family. For years Eugenia Grant ran one of the best pre-schools Basalt ever had. Within a few months after baby Alfred was born, Jens Peter was killed in a train accident around Cardiff in 1899. He and Anna are buried in Basalt today.

Walter Hyrup built another new house west of his own new one and Bus Ross and his family lived in it. Later, the Catholic Church used it for a social hall. Forrest Newkirk, my grandfather and an old railroad buddy of Walt Hyrup, used to take friends in that house with a tape measure and a T-square and chuckle at the slightly crooked walls. To the naked eye the house was beautiful. Joe Gregg, Jr. did the same thing as he gave me a tour of the old Tucker McClure house at Cap K Ranch. If ever a man knew his railroad stories, it was Walter Hyrup. The Basalt Regional Library has copies on file of many of his tales.

Pat Yale's father, Chris Hyrup, also worked for the Midland Railroad as a fireman until it went out of business in 1918. He then purchased the old Shehi place on the Frying Pan and went into farming on Taylor Creek. It was above where Jake and Julia Frieler lived. The Frielers' children were Bunny, Dottie and Barbara. Bunny lived in California for a while and came home once to visit. He had a souped-up Studebaker car. He bragged about both the Silver Hawk and the Golden Hawk. His was a Silver Hawk. He had put a larger Mercury engine in his smaller car and claimed he could "....outrun any highway patrolman in the State of California." It seems Bunny always had a love for fast cars.

Larry and Johnnie Hyrup's landmark home at Castle View. One of Larry's sons lives in it today.

Chris married Pat's mother, Hazel Mount, in 1914. She was Fanny Mount's only child. When they finally moved to Basalt, they lived in what was known as the Joe Hurtgen place on Second Street, formerly called County Road. Pat and three of her siblings were all born in that house. Mrs. Anna Olson was the midwife for all four of Chris Hyrup's children. Grandmother Fanny Mount was the first in the family to live in that house. Staying with Fanny, Pat and her siblings went to school in Basalt. On the weekends, holidays and in the summers they retreated quickly to the ranch on the Frying Pan. Doc Schweppe, whom we have mentioned elsewhere, bought the upper ranch and beautiful meadows when Chris Hyrup's health began to give out. This forced him to move to Basalt where he built a lovely log home on the hill above the Methodist Church.

I believe I had a crush on Chris' daughter Pat when we worked together at the Basalt Sundry. She was an extra bubbly sort of person that wore a perpetual smile. She was very fast on her feet and most efficient behind the soda fountain. She could work rings around us. In high school she was excellent at sports. Her siblings, all born in the Hurtgen house, were: Eugene (Dutch), Annabelle and Robert. Robert was once in a serious wreck with another Basalt Sundry worker, George Cunningham. Their car left the road and went off that terrible precipice known as Shale Bluff near the Aspen airport. It was a wonder either of them survived. Bob had both his shoes knocked off and George cracked his sternum. He was in a body cast for weeks. He would beg the rest of us at the sundry not to touch his sore upper body. I distinctly remember that Bob Hyrup served in the military.

Walter Hyrup was one of the most popular persons to ever live in Basalt. In addition to being a railroad worker, he operated a stone quarry on the Frying Pan. He also served as town marshal and was one of the best storytellers in town. Walt married Eva Letey. Her sister married Albert Grange and lived where Guido Myers had a tree farm. The Letey family once owned the ranch that Albert Grange took over. Walt and Eva once lived out there too. Their children were John V., who married Phyllis Bowles; JoAnne, who married Ervin Grant; Eugenia, who married Ervin's brother Don Grant; and Mary Rose, who married Harold Peuser. Ervin and Donald were the children of Ervin Sr. and Wilda Grant.

Otto Hyrup once signed papers to help his cousin Peter Anderson immigrate from Denmark. Peter worked for Larry Hyrup in the sawmill. He later worked for Berthoud Motors in Glenwood, as did his brother Hans Anderson who was sponsored in this country by Berthoud Motors. Peter Anderson married a Mennonite girl from Glenwood. Her name was Emma Jane and they had two sons. They retired and passed away in Arizona. The Mennonites have continually run the Valley View Hospital in Glenwood Springs. Faye Hyrup and Lloyd Fuhriman also lived on the ranch with Otto.

Seven Castles and Teddy Roosevelt

One of the claims to fame, of which the Midland Railroad boasted, was to have brought President Teddy Roosevelt over the Continental Divide, down the Frying Pan Valley, through Basalt and into Glenwood and New Castle in 1905. A huge reception was held for him in New Castle and the whole area turned out. President Roosevelt rode around on his horse with a few aides. His train was befittingly festooned with colorful presidential trappings.

Seven Castles was the second-most popular scenic stop on the Midland route, exceeded only by the dazzling precipice at Hell Gate. It is fairly certain that while passing Hell Gate they let the distinguished visitor out for a "look-

Seven Castles Creek muddies the Frying Pan River during a downpour. The worst cloudbursts in the entire valley came down here.

see." They may have stopped again at Seven Castles for him to take in that wonder of nature. We are glad it was not raining hard when he stopped at Seven Castles. He might have experienced one of the areas cloudbursts or "gully-washers." They surely can come down with ferocity. They have been known to wash out complete irrigation systems. They have moved tons of rock and dirt and even washed out large wooden bridges from their moorings. They have fouled up the Frying Pan road and plugged up the river. They have eroded the far bank and made the river run red for days. We have wondered how the fish can breathe or find their food. Surely, there are no worse places on the Frying Pan for these dramatic flash floods! With a combination of porous rocky red soil that washes out easily and a lack of foliage to hold back the torrents, this spot has to be the worst headache of all for the road crews. Even when there are no cloudbursts, the little Seven Castles Creek can muddy up the Frying Pan River all by itself.

Basalt was quite disappointed that Teddy Roosevelt did not come out of his private car. In Glenwood Springs he stayed in the Hotel Colorado, which boasted of having its lower extremities made from Frying Pan Peach Blow sandstone. One of the nicer rooms in the hotel, among the 200 rooms, is still called the Roosevelt Room to this day. As Teddy looked across the river toward the Glenwood train depot, he would have seen more Frying Pan stone on that

Pullman dining room. 1898.

building. Teddy had come to this area to do some serious hunting, including bear. He also rode his horse over the mountains to the Redstone area and stayed in that famous mansion. We heard that he bagged about six bears.

In spite of the danger for flooding, Seven Castles is becoming quite a popular spot for home building. Every time one drives past he sees evidence of a growing community in this much-preferred spot. Our good friend Mrs. Marie Bowman, frequent visitor to the Senior Citizen events in Basalt, probably built there due to its scenic nature and its proximity to good shopping and social events in Basalt. Mrs. Bowman's home was quite close to the former home of dearly-departed Doc and Bess Leonard. Glen and his wife Bess may have been among the most-loved summer visitors to the Frying Pan. The popular fish fries he sponsored in the Thomasville fire station have perpetuated for him an everlasting reputation for all who tasted that delicious seafood.

The Leonards were originally from Oklahoma. They first built a large home between Basalt and El Jebel. Cliff Elmont helped them build it and they became fast friends. The Leonards would spend the winters deep-sea fishing off the coasts of Texas. They would freeze the catch and ship it to the Frying Pan in the summer. Many helpful hands helped prepare it for consumption on large grills. The dinners were potluck. What tasty fare we all sampled! The crowd usually varied between 150 and 200 people. The "chit chat" was delightful. Among their other children, Doc and Bess had a lovely daughter named JoAnn who lived in the vicinity of Greeley. She was present at many of her father's fish fries. The lady minister from the Community Methodist Church of both Basalt and Thomasville would say "grace" and we would enjoy the meal. It was truly a "feather in one's cap" to say "I went to Doc's fish fry." (Kind of like being invited to the White House.) Regretfully, both of the Leonards have passed away. Their grandchildren still maintain a cabin at Meredith for summer enjoyment, but the home at Seven Castles has been sold. The Leonards were certainly part of the local color of the Frying Pan.

It appears to be a source of pride for a valley resident to say: "I climbed that large castle right there once." I wish I were a geologist like my second cousin in Toledo, Ohio. She is a great granddaughter of the famous Emery Arbaney. She could tell us if the similar formations on the way to Snowmass are part of Seven Castles. If one looks to the left while going to Aspen he will see siblings to the Seven Castles. Perhaps, eons of time ago, the Snowmass ones became separated from the mother formations by the eternal coursing of the Frying Pan River. At one time in our history there must have existed a great inter-mountain lake. The strata at Seven Castles and elsewhere testify to this. A sign at the top of the ski course above old Aspen declares that Mt. Sopris, near Carbondale, is only thirty-five thousand years old. I would have presumed it to be millions of years old. Perhaps, back when Mt. Sopris was spewing forth tons and tons of molten rock and Basalt Mountain was firing back with volley after volley of black basalt rock, the lake disappeared and the castles continued forming as millennia of wind and rain took a toll on them.

Basalt Mountain (formerly called Black Mountain), if viewed from the east as one is descending the Frying Pan, appears to be the head in profile of a giant gorilla. Speaking of rock formations and Seven Castles, my brother Cliff would never forgive me if I failed to mention "Yogi Bear." As one views the very first castle coming from the east, (and one has to look very quickly), you will see Yogi. He is quite small and stands on the forefront of that first easternmost castle. See if you can find him without causing a traffic pileup for the cars behind you. (And this from the Elmonts who also named Barney Google Rock.) Oh, how I wish the Eagle County Commissioners would let me place a road sign pointing up to Barney Google! It will require an old-timer to remember who Barney Google was in the comic strips. Going east, just a ways past Downey Creek, there is a tall red sandstone formation on the left side of the road. It is about a mile before one comes to the verdant fields of Cap K Ranch. Though the base of the formation is quite square and plain, up above one can clearly see the chin, lips, nose and cap of old Barney Google. (Lynn Nichols and Joe Gregg, have you seen him?) If one looks even

Barney Google Rock.

closer, he can see his "goog-goog-googly eyes." The best way to photograph him is to be headed westward on a clear day with a bright blue sky above. Stop just short of the formation, without causing a wreck, and frame his cute little head in the blue backdrop. We could even say he is a redhead.

I love to see an occasional Indian teepee at Seven Castles. Speaking of "teepees", did you hear the joke about the old Indian chief that drank seventeen cups of tea before retiring to bed? They found him drowned the next morning in his "tea pee." (Tee hee!) I love a good joke! Teepees are reminders of those

One of the Seven Castles.

hardy native Americans who lived in the area before it was even known as Frying Pan town. They were mostly Utes. Chief Colorow was one of their local leaders. The government used the Meeker Massacre as an excuse to run them off. They were relocated to the Uintah Basin near Vernal, Utah. It is said that the American Indians are the only people to have been defeated by the U.S. Government that did not come out ahead in the end. What a misnomer when Columbus called them "Indians", thinking he had found a new passage to India. We'll forgive him. In those days the only known continents were Europe, Africa and Asia. A giant land mass like America was still know as "islands of the sea" and the earth was still "flat." They say such injustices happen in the name of "progress." I still feel a great tinge of sadness when I think about such things. The Utes once camped right where the charcoal ovens sit in Basalt today. Every once in a while a lucky finder uncovers an arrowhead or other artifact. Bob Terrell, the former game warden, was very good at finding them and had quite a collection. Perhaps his only surviving son Dale has inherited it today.

I found it humorous, while researching this book, that Seven Castles only had one little tiny "water closet." No other railroad building existed there. Well, that's better than nothing! Suppose Teddy Roosevelt got off there to use it? Or did he refuse to come out like he did in Basalt? He probably had his own fancy toilet right in his private railroad car. The mention of a water closet brings to mind one of the funniest anecdotes I have ever heard. A woman had bought a ranch in the wild and wooly West, "sight unseen." (Let's say it happened at

Seven Castles a hundred years ago.) She had forgotten to ask the agent if there was a WC (water closet) on the property. Often communications go awry. He thought she was referring to W. C. (the Wesleyan Church). He replied: "Our W. C. is getting bigger every year. We don't know how we will fit the scores of people in. We only go to it once a week on Sundays. We can accommodate over sixty people at one time at the present. We have installed new plush velvet seats. Talk about 'commode', the French word for 'comfort.' It gives my bottom a most pleasant sensation. Some families like to bring a picnic lunch and make a day of it. Men and women enjoy sitting side by side with little children and speaking in whispers. Old hymn books are close at hand for our personal use. People really praised our facility when we installed air-conditioning and I noticed the smell improved somewhat too. It pains me not to be able to go more than once a week but I will just have to get used to it. I look forward to sitting right by your side at our W. C. the first time you come here. You will soon find the place familiar. Let's make it a family affair. Perhaps you could bring a chocolate cake. Be sure to dress properly for the occasion. Cordially, your agent."

Rocky Mountain Bighorn Sheep live in the Seven Castles area. Not too long ago, some of our best specimens were taken to Utah to improve their herd, while some of their scraggly ones were brought here for improvement. One day a ram came to visit Doc Leonard's home on the upper edge of Seven Castles. Doc had shiny green metal siding on his home. The ram saw his reflection in the siding and determined it was a rival. He made six or seven dents in the siding before moving on. The dents are still there (kind of like a status symbol on the home). The new owner, Mark Peppers, was kind enough to let me photograph them. Next, the naughty ram went a couple of houses away and saw

his image in a double sliding-glass door. Thinking it was another rival, he proceeded to break the glass. In the same vicinity a deer crashed through one large window, meandered through the house and exited via another big window. Golly, Marie Bowman, it was dangerous to live in your area. I hope you all had glass insurance.

Dents in the side of Doc Leonard's home at Seven Castles caused by a Rocky Mountain bighorn sheep who saw his reflection in the metal.

It can also be peaceful in Seven Castles. In the summer of 2002 I was driving up near Marie and Doc's homes when I saw what I was sure were chukar partridges. I had been told years earlier by game warden Bob Terrell that the chukar was the fastest game bird alive. He had helped to introduce them to the Frying Pan from Hungary in the 1950s. He once told me they can fly in excess of 55 miles per hour. I sensed rather quickly that these "fatties" were not chukars. They were not only slow, they far preferred to avoid me than to fly away. After photographing them I found out they were guinea fowl. Later I saw a flock of wild turkeys on the way up to Doctor Schweppe's ranch at the top of Taylor Creek. They certainly did not want me to photograph them and were experts at camouflage. I concluded that our beloved Frying Pan is a paradise for various and ample wildlife.

The river itself has to be one of the premier fly-fishing streams in all of America. I find groups of six and eight and twelve fishing in the same spot. I have seen women with their husbands "drowning worms" and entire families sharing a rock or two. I have jokingly said, "You need to bring your own rock if you plan to fish on the Frying Pan." I asked one fisherman, in the summer of 2002, where he was from. He replied that he lived in Lawrence, Kansas. I asked how he became aware of the Frying Pan River. He replied, "Every fisherman worth his salt knows about the Frying Pan." Word of mouth apparently is our best advertisement.

We warned you to "bring your own rock" to sit on. Here an entire family fishes on the Frying Pan River.

Mr. Whit McClelland of Ponte Vedra, Florida, sent me the following quote from Teddy Roosevelt. It seems appropriate to reproduce it here: "It is not the critic who counts; not the man who points out how the strong man stumbled, or where the doer of the deed could have done better. The credit belongs to the man who is actually in the arena; whose face is marred by dust, sweat and blood; who strives valiantly; who errs and comes short again and again...because there is no effort without error and shortcoming.

It is the man who does actually strive to do the deeds; who knows the great enthusiasm; the great devotions; who spends himself in a worthy cause; who at the best knows in the end the triumph of high achievement... And who at the worst, if he fails, at least fails while daring greatly, so that his place shall never be with those cold and timid souls who know neither victory nor defeat."

Taylor Creek and That Generous Doc. Schweppe

Though we all called him "Doc", that philanthropic Mr. Schweppe was really John Shedd Schweppe and his wife was Lydia Elliott Schweppe. Their children are Leigh, Charles and David. Leigh (Buettner) of Colorado Springs, was most helpful to me in the publication of this book. The Schweppes had six grandchildren. They came from Lake Forest, Illinois, and he was a specialist in cancer research.

Doc first learned about the Frying Pan from his brother-in-law in Glenwood Springs, who owned the International Harvester Distributorship. Doc bought what was the old Shehi place and, later, Chris Hyrup's ranch above Taylor Creek. I must say I don't know if there is a prettier place on the whole Frying Pan. I guess Cap K Ranch would tie for second place in scenic beauty. When I first saw the gorgeous meadows at the top of Taylor Creek, I was sort of awe-struck. There were three or four lovely homes up there, one of which was Doc Schweppe's. My brother,

The lovely meadows at the top of Taylor Creek.

Cliff, claims the distinction of having helped to build Doc's guest house and pool with the help of Forrest Hendricks and Glen Spaulding. Cliff used to work for Horace Hendricks, one of the foremost builders of homes and businesses in Aspen. Doc had an attractive tennis court right below his house.

On the way up there I saw a flock of wild turkeys. I never really truly sensed how completely wonderful the Frying Pan watershed is and what a marvelous habitat it is for wildlife. On one side of the road past Doc Schweppe's house, I saw horses grazing. On the other side, cattle contentedly chewed their cuds. A lovely little girl gave me directions as she peddled down the dirt lane on her bicycle. She is the one who told me which one was Doc Schweppe's house. How lovely it must have been for Doc Schweppe to come there for a rest when the cares of the world in his more demanding profession weighed down heavily upon him. How much his wife and children must have enjoyed that special paradise up there. How private and remote it was from the bustling workaday world.

Doc Schweppe was a true philanthropist in the finest sense of the word. He used his money as early as 1947 to establish a family foundation to provide

research fellowships to M.D.'s and Ph.D.'s. It is still operating today under the auspices of his children. Doc loved bird hunting, fishing, golf and travel. The ranch was mostly a place for his family to be together. The cattle ranching was only a hobby.

Doc died of a heart attack in his sleep in 1996. He will be greatly missed always

The home of the famous philantropist, Dr. Schweppe, at the top of Taylor Creek. It is perhaps the most scenic and peaceful spot on the entire Frying Pan.

by his family and friends. One of his friends worked for him for over thirty years as a housekeeper. Her name was Jenny Arlian of Sopris Village. She was the sister of my aunt, Linda Nelson. The Schweppes were always so good to Jenny and she loved them dearly. When Jenny died recently, the kind Schweppes donated a large and beautiful aquarium to the Heritage Park Care Center in Carbondale where Jenny spent her last years. The plaque on the aquarium says: "In Memory of Jenny Arlian. The Schweppe Family."

There are some attractive residences at the bottom of Doc Schweppe's little valley called Taylor Creek. I believe one group of them is known as the J-L Ranch. Here also the famous Virginia Hinderliter used to live. She is mentioned elsewhere in this book in the section about Smith Creek.

Downey Creek and That Marvelous Mr. Peter Jouflas

On Downey Creek, just west of the Cap-K Ranch, sits the former home of Mr. and Mrs. Peter Jouflas. Someone has beautifully remodeled it since its former days. Peter George Jouflas was born in Mavrolitharion, Greece, in 1886. His wife, Dionisia (Dorothy) Anadiotis, was born in 1898 in Amalias, Greece. He passed away in 1957. She died in 1972. They are both buried in Grand Junction, Colorado, home of their son Chris and their grandson, also named Chris, who is a prominent veterinarian in that community. They have another son, George Peter Jouflas. His brother Chris reports that George has done very well in life like his father. Humility keeps Chris from saying how he has done. It is Chris who has been so helpful to the author in reporting on his illustrious father.

Peter started in the sheep ranching business in the Price-Helper area in 1910. In addition to the ethnic Greeks, there were some Basque sheepherders in that area too, from Spain. In 1914 he bought land in the Piñon Mesa area of Mesa County. It was around 1918 when he purchased his first land on Downey Creek in the Frying Pan River Valley. His were among the very first sheep herds in Eagle County. He leased a forest permit on the Red Table Mountain extending as far east as Last Chance Creek. In 1926 he bought a homestead on Ute Creek near Wolcott, Colorado. In the 1930s he bought four more adjoining homesteads on Cache Creek, also in Eagle County. In total, he owned over 2,500 contiguous acres. In 1945 he purchased an adjoining ranch in Wolcott from the Holland brothers. This ranch consisted of 4,000 acres and included two forest permits. One was called Game Creek. Today that permit is a key part of the Vail ski area. All told Mr. Jouflas owned approximately 7,500 acres in the Wolcott/Vail area. When he purchased land in the Vail area, he might as well have purchased high producing gold mines. The land became extremely valuable. It has been estimated that Peter Jouflas was a multi-millionaire at the time of his death. Surely, his family would scoff at the highest estimates we have heard floating around (three hundred million dollars). His winter range was in Utah between Cisco and Thompson not far from the Colorado border. It is said that high grade oil was discovered on the land increasing the value of his holdings. He owned a homestead there in Water Canyon of 640 acres. His ranch held one of the original grazing permits under the Taylor Grazing Act.

He sold the Frying Pan ranch in 1946 to Tucker McClure who eventually owned practically all of the Frying Pan Valley. In 1947 Peter purchased properties on the outskirts of Grand Junction. The property is now in the middle of town and is considered "....some of the best property in Grand Junction." It is still in the family and, according to some, includes areas of what is now the famous North Avenue. Mr. Jouflas left the Frying Pan because he was running sheep in two areas. He found it more opportune to consolidate his efforts into one large outfit running 4-5,000 ewes. He was a hard-working, honest immigrant from Greece with little formal education. He was known by many as "....the king of the Greeks." He helped many ethnic friends and others get started in the sheep business. His family still owns the land at Wolcott, where his granddaughter owns the Wolcott Store. The family has likewise hung onto the properties at Grand Junction and in Utah.

Peter Jouflas' Greek Orthodox Religion was an integral part of his life. He was a man who had many friends and who always was willing to extend a helping hand to someone in need. He was a gentle man with great humility. When he came to America in 1907 he had little money, no skills in the English language and no training in business. But, through honest hard work and great perseverance, he built one of the best livestock operations in Colorado. His business spanned the great depression, which was a time when many lost everything they owned. He not only held his outfit together, but slowly acquired more land in the Wolcott area in the thirties and helped many others start their own sheep outfits during that period in his life. He once said to my brother, Fred, while still on the Frying Pan, "Dey yust tink I am a dumb old Greek. But I vil show dem. Someday I vil be richer dan dem all!" How prophetic his statement was! His story has to be one of the most remarkable to ever come out of the Frying Pan. I could have quoted Mr. Jouflas in ordinary well-spoken English, but his son Chris agreed with me that he didn't speak that way. Not quoting him exactly the way he talked would rob all the charm that filled his voice. He was, as Mark Twain would say, "part of the local color" of the Frying Pan and Eagle valleys.

His fellow Greeks, the Terliamis family of Sopris Creek, walked their sheep all the way to Lake Ivanhoe each summer.

Mr. Johnny Hyrup, now of Parachute, Colorado, knew Mr. Jouflas on the Frying Pan. He visited their home on Downey Creek. He said the Jouflases were short people. Johnny is no giant himself, but he said he had to duck to get in Peter's front door. They were just as amiable to him as my brother reported them to be. Johnny says they had a red sandstone oven in their back yard. This is a very European custom. No one with any sense likes to bake bread or cook a roast indoors on a hot summer day.

I had seen these types of ovens in my nearly three-year stay in Argentina. May I describe them and their ingenious method of construction to the reader? One first builds a platform for the oven to rest on. It should be waist high to avoid stooping. Next, one builds the actual oven with stones and mud or bricks and mud. I suppose cement would also suffice as mortar. The oven, when finished, resembles a large egg with the widest end down. In the front is a small metal door. Some preliminary wood fires are built in the oven to harden the mortar. Then, while the mother makes the dough in the kitchen sink with flour up to her elbows and in her hair and on her apron, the father builds a super

The magnificent Cap K Ranch on the Frying Pan as seen from the High Line Road above Downey Creek.

giant fire in the oven. When the wood burns down to embers, he scoops the fire out and wipes the bottom of the oven with a large clean rag on the end of a stick. Out comes the mother with the dough and plops it in on the clean hot oven floor. In some big round loaves she puts cinnamon and raisins. In others she may add cooked bacon bits. Timing the perfectly risen dough with the flawless oven temperature, she closes the oven door and waits. She never has to worry about timing or about burning the bread. When the bricks are so cool that they won't cook anymore, the bread is done to perfection. The kitchen sink is employed because usually enough bread is made to last a week or more. A bowl would never suffice. For the same reasons, the author often buys specialty breads in stores today. I have never tasted such delicious bread in my entire lifetime.

Mr. and Mrs. Peter Jouflas, though you are gone, we take our hats off to you. Had we known you and been privileged to live around you like some were, I am sure we would have learned a thing or two and we would have loved you! To think that portions of Peter's land have become parts of the busiest ski resort in America today! Vail is the favorite resort of former President Gerald Ford. He is skiing where that marvelous Mr. Peter Jouflas once walked. Peter, you would be proud to know that your descendants, full-blooded Americans, are honoring your name today. Rest in peace! (Que en paz descanse!)

We close with a story that many claim happened to themselves, but in reality it really did happen to the Jouflas family. They were on their way to Denver and stopped at a stockyard in Avon. Lo and behold, there was one of their ewes in a pen. They were driving the family car, a Cadillac sedan and, over the family objections, Peter told them to put the ewe in the back seat of the car so they could take her back to the ranch. The family objected strenuously but Peter replied: "This ewe bought this car and she can buy us another one!" They did as they were told!

Cap K Ranch and Tucker McClure

Long before young Tucker McClure ever came to the Frying Pan area, he had an uncle whose last name was "Tucker" that ran sheep near North Fork and Savage Lake. Young Tucker got his given name from that uncle. Tucker came as often as he could in the summertime to help with the sheep. He must have fallen in love with the area because, after amassing a fortune in several ventures around the world, he came home to build a house, buy a ranch and stay.

The U. S. Government was helping with a lot of construction in Panama, Ecuador, the Galapagos Islands and elsewhere. Several construction companies in America went together to form a giant conglomerate to do the work. Latin America had lots of native labor to do the work, but were short on experienced men to run the big machinery. Albert Nelson, the author's uncle, had done a lot of construction for an elderly man named Switzer. They built the road from Sylvan Lake near Eagle, to Woods Lake near Lime Park. This road was built almost entirely by horse-drawn equipment, plows, rippers, and scrapers. Considerable blasting powder was used. Much hand labor went into the effort. Then they moved over by Delta, Colorado, and built the Switzer Reservoir and more roads. By then horses were out of the picture and nice heavy-duty power equipment was in. Mr. Nelson had become quite skilled in his work when he answered an ad in a California newspaper seeking employees of Albert's type for overseas work. The Company was called Swinterman, McClure and Venell. They sent Albert to the Galapagos Islands to run bulldozers and other big equipment. Albert in turn sent for his younger brother Earl Nelson to come down and help. Earl joined him in the Galapagos and later in Ecuador, head-quartered in Guayaquil. McClure's company did well and McClure came back to the Frying Pan millions of dollars richer and started buying up land from farmers and ranchers who were most eager to sell. The earlier depression and the war years had put many ranchers in a bind. The Sloss brothers, for instance, were about to lose both their ranches and their cattle. Mr. McClure was a "lifesaver" for them.

Tucker McClure stayed in the upper story of the old brick Stirling P. Sloss home that still stands there today. Stirling was the father of twins, Alfred and

The lovely home that Stirling P. Sloss built for his wife. Now part of the Cap K Ranch.

Alvin. Alfred later moved to Basalt and became an Eagle County Commissioner. His brother, Alvin, retired to Glenwood Springs. Stirling built the lovely brick home as a gift for his wife. He petitioned for a post office at his ranch. It was approved and the railroad moved its office from Peach Blow to Sloss when the post office was approved. The old Midland Depot, one of the few left, still sits across the road south from the big two-story brick home. One cannot view it and its hand-painted sign near the roof without experiencing *déja vu* and nostalgia. My roots are there and my heart is turned each year to Basalt and the Frying Pan.

McClure was busy building himself a new stone home up near the foothills above the old Sloss place. Mr. Joe Gregg, Jr., lives in it today. Otmar Lucksinger of Basalt was the first person to live and ranch at what is Cap K today. Stirling P. Sloss, who went by "Price", bought the place from Otmar. Stirling was a most enterprising man. He started the Frying Pan Stockgrower's Association. He led the fight to eradicate the larkspur menace in Lime Park's summer pastures. Larkspur is deadly to cattle. Price's son, Alvin, ran the post office at Sloss until July 31, 1931.

Since early childhood, McClure had a good friend in Glenwood Springs by the name of Dr. Ould. He was a prominent dentist in the area and also became McClure's private attorney for purchasing large tracts of private land in the Frying Pan area. McClure also bought into the Big Four Ranch southeast of

The old Sloss Depot (earlier called Sloane). Alvin Sloss ran a post office in this building until 1939.

Carbondale, which had been owned by Clyde Gus, who had raised hay and grain on the property. Though living on the Frying Pan, McClure still had his fingers in many South American adventures. He found himself once again enlisting workers to help in the Galapagos Islands. This time Frank Crowley went down to help and so did Russel Noren from a big cattle ranch on Divide Creek.

When McClure first bought the Sloss Ranch, now Cap K, he asked Alvin Sloss to stay on and run it. The old Midland depot had long ago been shut down and Alvin and Clement Sloss were living in it. McClure also bought the Peter Jouflas ranch adjacent to his own on the west. He next bought the Williams Ranch at Meredith. Then he bought the Crowley ranches at Jakeman Creek, Deadman Creek and Bessie Park.

After a while Tucker became unhappy with the management of his main ranch. He sent Russel Noren back to the U. S. to manage all of his newfound ranches. After a couple of years Noren decided to move on. Walt Roberts managed things for a couple of years until McClure fired him. Then Jim Crowley began to manage the big Williams Ranch at Meredith. Soon Mr. McClure had Jim managing all the Frying Pan ranches. Crowley and his family moved into the big brick Sloss home. At that time his family consisted of his wife, Eulalia, and two girls, Lea and Frankie.

By now work had slowed considerably in the islands and most of the men came home. Earl Nelson, using his considerable skills with a Caterpillar, built the fish ponds that still exist on the Cap K Ranch. Tucker McClure at this time was spending most of his time at home on the ranch. He saw to most of the operation of the ranch and was comfortably snuggled into his new stone and log home up against the mountain. He next bought property at North Fork owned by John and Nel Irions. Cap K Ranch still owns that property and lake today.

Mrs. Crowley soon found herself cooking for a large crew of men and the McClure family and their friends as well. Jim was working long hours and they now had a new child, Betty. The Crowleys, feeling a little overwhelmed, pulled up stakes and moved to Basalt where they purchased the Frying Pan Inn, one of Basalt's original buildings. It came with a motel, a bar, a restaurant and a five-year lease. Once again the hours became too long for the family. Though they had an option to buy the place, they chose not to do such. From there they moved to the Diamond G Ranch (not to be confused with Diamond J) at Ruedi. They ran the ranch and tended the cattle for the McLaughlins. Crowleys loved their new job and stayed there until the Bureau of Reclamation took much of the land for the Ruedi Reservoir, which dates to 1965. Little Jimmy was born while the Crowleys lived at Diamond G. Now the parents had two half-grown children and two little babies.

The beautiful ponds on Cap K Ranch. The author's uncle, Earl Nelson, helped Tucker McClure build them.

It was less than a year from when the Crowleys left Mr. McClure's employ that Tucker had a heart attack and died. Within a year after that McClure's wife died. Their son came from California to the ranch to see if he wanted any of the belongings. He chose three favorite pictures off the walls and left the rest. Both McClure and his wife left money to the son.

The Nichols and Gregg families of Kansas City had been looking for a nice ranch in the mountains for some time. Allen McClure, the son, sold the ranch to the Nichols and Gregg families in 1955. From that moment it became the Cap K Ranch. Lynn Nichols, who lives in a large house on the property today, said her grandfather, R. B. Caldwell is the one who suggested naming the ranch after the wives in the family or "....It will never be a success." The name "Cap" was the first name of Joe Gregg's wife. "K" stood for "Katie", Miller Nichol's wife.

Lynn Nichols, daughter of Miller Nichols, is really Mrs. Jim Gilchrist. But, as often happens in business circles, an earlier name lingers on. She lives on the ranch and has done so since 1981. Their two sons, Carson and Griffin, live with them. She has offered great moral support to me as the author. I have coveted not only her home and her ranch, but her two beautiful llamas also. I am a semi-expert on llamas, having lived in South America. They are not afraid of any known predator. They have very sharp defensive hooves and know how to use them. They will run off a coyote. One of their best defensive mechanisms is to chew their cud, like a bovine, and then spit a dark awful solution that will never come out of a white shirt. It is reported by Argentines in the know that they can spit forty feet. So, if you stop along the wayside to snap a photo of one of Lynn's llamas, beware!

The sign at the Cap K Ranch, formerly the Tucker McClure and Sloss ranches.

Joe Gregg, Jr., living in the Tucker McClure home at the base of the hill, is one of the most affable souls a person would ever meet. He gave the author a full tour of the most interesting home built by McClure. We spent an hour or two in pleasant conversation. Though the house is quite nice, it is not without its faults. It was built by local valley help who had not yet completely honed their building skills. Mr. Gregg remarked that visitors sometimes smiled when it was pointed out that the walls were not exactly straight or flush. One of the more astonishing things is that the master bedroom is so small and has only a single bed in it. Mrs. McClure did not overly enjoy the house and stayed elsewhere. The only bed in there was Tucker's. Like all the main pieces of furniture in the house, the items were hand-carved in elegant patterns etched in Panama. The chairs, the tables, the couches, the lamps, the beds, all were hand-carved with little notches by skilled Panamanian hands. McClure had all the furniture shipped here.

While in Panama, McClure had lived in his own private elegantly furnished train car. It was hooked on to a Panamanian train and the local government did Tucker's bidding. His train car had very decorative lamps in it operated by gas. He had the lamps shipped home and switched to electricity throughout his new home. He had a beautifully carved mahogany mantle on his fireplace. It too had familiar carvings from Panama. In the middle of the mantle was a large spot without any decorations. One of Tucker's guests was the man who had drawn "Elsie" for the Borden Company. He asked Tucker if he would like an Elsie carved into the mantle. Tucker was delighted and "Elsie, the Borden Cow", has been there ever since. The reader is now in possession of some very interesting trivia never known before by most.

Tucker had a large and long back porch that led out to a red sandstone patio and huge stone barbeque grill. One day one of those famous Frying Pan flash floods came down the mountain and filled in the whole back porch and a couple of the back rooms of the house with debris. Mr. McClure was most unhappy and jumped into one of his own bulldozers, when nature permitted, and went up and completely rearranged Mother Nature's face. Never again did any flood bother that house. Mr. Gregg has had that long room enclosed with wood and glass and it now serves as an excellent dining room for guests…right off the kitchen.

I took Joe Gregg out to the front lawn to pose for a picture. He told me I was standing quite close to the old county High Line Road. He invited me to investigate the road. He pointed out how clever the road builders were, especially the manner in which they built the culverts. Fearing continual washouts from cloudbursts, they built sandstone culverts layer upon layer with an upward-arched capstone. In big gullies, these culverts were large enough to handle the sudden flow without washing out the road. In smaller gullies there was no capstone, just layer upon layer of sandstone through which the runoff trickled and went on

A sandstone culvert on the old CountyLine Road.

its way. The most any road grader ever had to do was grade the road above the culvert without having to replace any culverts. I have noticed a similar construction on the newer paved Frying Pan road. An "old dog" can certainly teach "new tricks." To survey this old road I had to disturb the peace and tranquility of several of Cap K's big old bulls and horses. I noticed massive power lines running along the old road. I felt I had met a true gentleman and a new friend in Joe Gregg, Jr.

Peach Blow, Hopkin's Spur and Blair

These three locations are next to each other on the Frying Pan. Peach Blow is closer to Basalt, whereas Blair and Hopkin's Spur lie a little bit more to the east. Peach Blow is not too far west of Sloss or Cap K Ranch. The quarry was very active in 1894. It was once the most famous red sandstone quarry in all of Colorado. Hopkin's Spur stone eventually became known as Peach Blow stone. When one arrives at a place where it is obvious someone did much digging in the red hillside, one is at Peach Blow. Peach Blow has no buildings near it and is at a wide turnout where fishermen love to park. Hopkin's Spur, a bit farther east, has no good parking spots that are not privately owned and has beautiful lodgings with well-done landscaping on the south side of the road. Do not confuse the two locations!

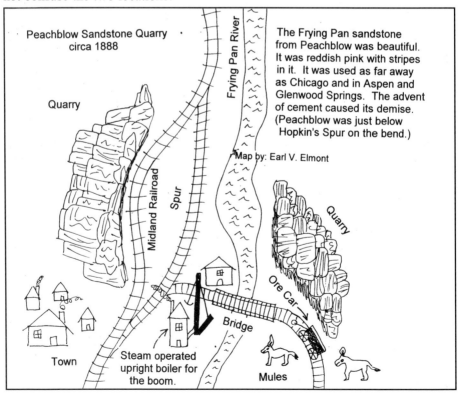

Peachblow Sandstone Quarry circa 1888

Quarry

Frying Pan River

The Frying Pan sandstone from Peachblow was beautiful. It was reddish pink with stripes in it. It was used as far away as Chicago and in Aspen and Glenwood Springs. The advent of cement caused its demise. (Peachblow was just below Hopkin's Spur on the bend.)

Map by: Earl V. Elmont

Midland Railroad

Spur

Quarry

Ore Car

Town

Steam operated upright boiler for the boom.

Bridge

Mules

Peach Blow was once a small town and quarrying took place on both sides of the river. It once had four or five buildings including a store, a post office and a school. Now they are all gone. Peach Blow once had its own train station which later moved east to Sloss, taking the post office along with it. Mr. Alvin Sloss managed to pull that off and ran the post office until 1931.

Hazel Mount, daughter of Fanny Mount and mother of Patricia Hyrup Yale, had the distinct honor and unique privilege of being a former student at the school. Her teacher was Roaldo D. Strong. Hazel later became the wife of Chris Hyrup and then became Patricia's mother. Pat made sure that I mention that her mother formerly went to that school. That is a distinction that only a handful of people can claim. Cliff Held once built a home on the site of the old Peach Blow school. It was due east of the White River National Forest sign on the Frying Pan Road.

Part of the famous Peachblow Quarry.

Peach Blow was earlier called Wilson's Quarries. When the railroad built a siding there, they must have felt they had the right to change the name to Peach Blow. Where they got that name is anyone's guess. Some of Mr. Wilson's workers were L. M. Larson, Gus Anderson, Adelbert Downey and Dave Hull. The quarry, as we have said, operated on both sides of the river. Going eastward, a siding took off to the right. The rock from the south side was transported via a small rail line with tiny tram cars pulled by horses or mules. The cars were pulled over a crude looking rickety bridge with one central support out in the middle of the river. From thence the stones were lifted onto flat cars via a tall wooden hydraulic boom powered by an upright steam boiler. Usually the boom operator was very careful not to damage any railroad cars, but one day he carelessly dropped a huge cut stone and pretty well smashed a box car which he had not noticed. In my imagination I can still hear voices of husky workers shouting directions here and there while the cutting saws "zinged" out their melodies and rock dust flew everywhere. I'll wager the railroad workers and the rock cutters vied to see who was the dirtiest by the end of the day.

The Glenwood Hot Springs Lodge was made of Frying Pan Peach Blow stone.

Mr. Wilson's red sandstone had beautiful colored streaks in it. Some were black and some were lighter. The stone became coveted all around the state and nation for building material. The places where it ended up are almost legendary. It is found in Leadville, Aspen, Glenwood Springs, Colorado Springs, Denver and as far away as Chicago. In Aspen it is found in the Wheeler Opera House, the Hotel Jerome, the Pitkin County Courthouse, from which the notorious James Bundy jumped, and in some of the older Aspen churches. It is found in Glenwood Springs in the railroad depot, the Hot Springs Lodge and Pool, and in the bottom layers of the Hotel Colorado. One customer in Chicago purchased 300,000 pieces of Peach Blow stone. Mr. Wilson must have exclaimed once: "Oh why did they have to invent cement and ruin my livelihood?" Cement was cheaper and easier to obtain. Goodbye to Peach Blow Quarry stone for a long time!

Near Peach Blow is the slightly less famous Hopkin's Spur. The lovely houses there today, especially those closest to the road, are owned by the same Mr. John Morris that owns the Frying Pan River Ranch at Nast. His able caretaker is Mr. Ken Lawyer. There is a well-carved sign over the driveway at Hopkin's Spur announcing the place. We all used to believe that Walt Hyrup quarried stone at Hopkin's Spur. But Pat Hyrup Yale says she went with her famous uncle a time or two to cut rock and that he always got it at Peach Blow. According to the Danielson brothers, in their great book, the stone usually carried the name "Peach Blow" even if it came from a different quarry.

Hopkin's Spur is not quite as famous for some reason as the location known as Blair. One could throw a stone west from Hopkin's Spur and hit the ground where silver-haired Frank and Annie Blair once lived. Their house was long and narrow because it was squeezed in against the mountain and the railroad track south of it.

The remains of Annie Blair's chicken coop.

Annie, known affectionately by all who knew her, was called "Mother Blair." Besides raising some chickens, she was a famous cook. Remnants of her chicken coop still lie in the brush on the north side of the road. The legends about her chickens and her chicken dinners traveled far and wide. She first accused the train engineers of scaring her chickens when they tooted their whistles and "....ran all the fat off my chickens." It is said she stood in the tracks one day and physically stopped the train. She offered a Sunday chicken dinner if those railroad engineers would quit scaring her chickens. They agreed to the deal. This story was told to me by my brother Bill who helped build Chapman Dam with the CCC Camp. He knew the Blairs personally. Annie also made three or more kinds of homemade pie. The railroad workers couldn't wait to buy them. They were apple, raspberry (perhaps "wild") and thimbleberry. I had never heard of thimbleberry pie. It almost sounded like something out of Hansel and Gretel. The railroad workers soon paid cash for the pies or exchanged them for piles of coal for Annie.

Frank Blair was the railroad line watchman in that area. It was his job to walk the line from Blair to the current site of Ruedi Dam. He watched for boulders and loose track. Once, in modern times, my brother, Cliff, was driving from his home in Meredith to Basalt. He reached the vicinity below the Ruedi Dam when he noticed a giant rock slide coming down the mountain side right toward him. It had been triggered by a recent rain. He said the boulders were the size of his Bronco II car. Where was Frank Blair when Cliff needed him to watch out for boulders? (In the Basalt Fairview Cemetery with his beloved wife, Annie.) Cliff felt inspired to jump out and run for safety. The enormous boulders landed all around him but did not touch his car. One big rock left a three foot deep impression in the black top. Cliff noticed that there was just enough room between two boulders to extricate his car. He drove to Hopkin's Spur to borrow a phone. There is a cute little pond there with a spray coming up out of the center of it. Cliff did not set his brake well and, while he was on the phone to warn the highway department, his car rolled into the pond. It cost him $100 to tow it out.

On another occasion, just west of the boulder incident, a huge buck deer came up out of the river with no warning and put a four inch dent in Cliff's driver's door. He also broke the mirror loose and caught it in his horns and tore all the black coloration off his nose. Months later I found a birthday card for him with a big buck on it. I took "white out" and removed the black off the buck's nose and, using a small piece of metallic cardboard off a package of cold medicine, I fashioned a little mirror and glued it into the buck's horns. Cliff said he loves that card and still saves it. But he does not cherish the memory of that big buck.

One book said that it is entirely possible that the Blairs were the most well-loved family in all the annals of railroad history. The Midland Railroad workers found every excuse in the world to stop there. One fireman on one of the trains said the coal in his tender was too heavy and he had to lighten it to prevent damage. He left a huge pile for Annie Blair. Another engineer said he had to stop and rest his train for the "long climb" to Basalt. It was so flat between Blair and Basalt that the train could have coasted all the way without moving the throttle. It is said that Mrs. Blair always liked to make cute little expressions when she found the coal. "Do you suppose a train wrecked here losing some of its coal? Oh, my!" I felt some real nostalgia when I passed their graves in Basalt knowing that I had missed out on a golden opportunity to have known some truly wonderful people. Maybe next time!

Frank and Annie Blair's home once stood along the tracks where the curved arrow sign now stands. Homes at Hopkin's Spur are visible on the right.

Livestock Brands on the Frying Pan

WH Walter Hyrup.

⋏ John Smith and sons, Phil and Cliff, Toner Creek, now the Game
And Fish Ranch.

つ△ Otto Hyrup and son Larry, Seven Castles Ranch.

CHC Chris Hyrup, Taylor Creek, now the Schweppe Ranch.

Pↄ Jake Freiler, Taylor Creek, Virginia Hindenlighter.

O Alfred Sloss, Otto Creek.

PJ Peter Juflas, Downey Creek, now Cap-K Ranch, formerly
Tucker McClure Ranch.

O Stirling P. Sloss and sons, Alvin and Alfred. Frenchman Creek.

T⅃ Then Tucker McClure Ranch, now Cap-K Ranch.

HB Harvey Biglow, Ruedi Creek, Sharp Brothers.

Ψ Bob Reed, then.....

Ⓔ Peter Englebrecht, then Fred McLaughlin, Diamond G Ranch.

T.I Fred McLaughlin.

JC Jones and Crowley, Huffman Ranch, then Diamond G Ranch,
John Clay, Bill Groves, Joe Hurtgen, McLaughlin, Pond Creek,
Part of Diamond G.

T.I Fred McLaughlin Brand, Ruedi and Pond Creek.

FN Frank Neil, Ruedi Creek.

BS Bill Smith, Ruedi and Smith Creek.

JG Joe Goddard, Smith Creek, Dr. Jackson, Trump, Sharp Brothers.

EN Leon Nelson, Swan Nelson, Freeman Creek.

FF Fred Williams Family, Miller Creek, then Tucker McClure, now Cap-K Ranches, Bureau of Reclamation Reservoir.

HD Augustine Dearhamer, Howard Dearhamer, Meredith Store and Post Office, now Dearhamer Campground.

PB Paul Billow and sons, Herman and Fred, now Bureau of Recla-Mation, Meredith, 2 x 4 Creek.

NO BRAND F. D. Newkirk, Waterbury Creek, (Howard and Poreth) then (Woolley) then Pender, Meredith Store and trailers, Woolley, Doc Leonard, Bonnie Williams, Jakeman Creek Ranch.

S John Schneider, Jakeman Creek, then Claude Crowley Ranches, then Tucker McClure, then Cap-K.

S Crowley Ranches, Thomasville, Deadman Creek, Nelson Gulch, Suicide Gulch, Middle Gulch, Bessie Park, Swinford Ranch, then Thompson, then Crowley, then Tucker McClure, then Cap-K Ranches.

I L I George McLaren, Lime Creek, Calcium, now Dearhamer, (Ridge-Way) (White) (Cashman) Roy Lee Williams (Ellen)

E Peter Englebrecht and son, Paul, Woods Lake Resort, then (Luthey?), (Bowles Brothers) John Denver, Art Pfister and others Of Aspen, D.C. Coffield (part of Biglow Ranch)

J Diamond J Ranch, Bowles Brothers, Bruce Riley, (Simms) and Coombs.

HB Harvey Biglow, North Fork, Lumsden, Tooney, Swamley Co. Ranch, (De Haven) Biglow. Darwin & Roberta Caulfield,

Ψ North Fork Ranch, Bob Reed, Nell Irions, old house still there. (Historic place.)

NC Norrie Colony, Norrie, Lamont, Jameson, Whitbeck, Falk, Clyde Vagneur, Lamont Ranch was Dorothy Falk's.

CS Clyde Swisher (Hawthorne) Nast, (Frying Pan River Ranch), Craig Coombs.

Ruedi To Biglow

Ruedi

When John Ruedi and Otmar Lucksinger sold all their Basalt land, they simultaneously moved to the current site of Ruedi in about 1880. The author's relatives, the Jonce Houghs, moved there at about the same time from the east. They settled on 220 acres north of Mr. Ruedi on land just about where Fred McLaughlin later settled, in the vicinity of the current large Ruedi Campgrounds. Several owners had the land before Mr. McLaughlin, a state representative, finally bought it and established his Diamond G Guest Ranch.

The original John Ruedi homestead.

John Ruedi's house was 15-foot square. He sold his land to H. L. Ford and a Mr. Henderson. Ford was the Midland agent at Colorado Springs and wanted a ranch on the Frying Pan, so he bought at Ruedi. His family supplied all the fresh fish to the Colorado Midland dining cars. Ford and Henderson sold to Frank Neal, father of Richard Neal who lives in Thomasville today. Mr. Ruedi once had 720 acres of land. Fred Shehi at one time lived in Ruedi and later moved to Basalt. Mrs. Irondale lived in the center of Ruedi just below the old school. Sam Phillips and his wife had seven kids. He and Ray Jones were patrolmen for the Midland. Percy Blodgett lived in Ruedi and married Richard Neal's grandmother, Bertha Neal. There was a large Smith Hotel just below the old school. It was owned by Bill Smith who lived on Smith Creek. Ruedi's famous horseshoe lakes used to be riverbed for the Frying Pan River as it curved through the valley.

Ruedi was never a large town, nor were its railroad facilities expansive. There were some nice homes, a huge plaster factory, a train depot and a school. Dances were held twice a year in the old Ruedi School. The desks and other furniture were carried outside to make room for the dancers. The railroad had a spur which led up to the plaster factory. A few people lived in tents which are visible in the old photos. The Frying Pan made two huge horseshoe bends as it

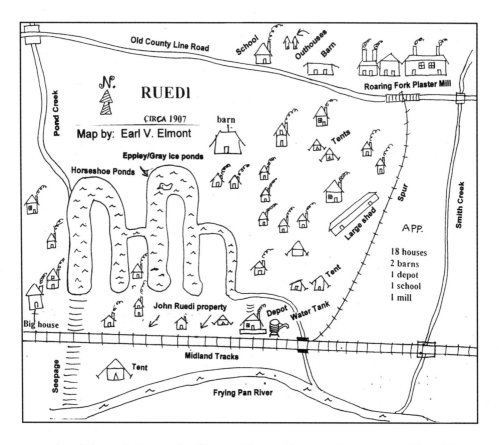

RUEDI

CIRCA 1907

Map by: Earl V. Elmont

18 houses
2 barns
1 depot
1 school
1 mill

meandered through the north of town. The ponds were the source of Basalt's ice in the winter, courtesy of Bill Gray and the Eppley family. Some of the more prominent families who lived there were: the Sam Phillips, the Swan and Leon Nelsons, the Frank Neals and (earlier) the John Ruedis, the Jonce Houghs, the Vandeventers, the Curtises and the Percy Blodgetts. A "guesstimate" from an old photo indicates that Ruedi once had about 18 homes and a few large barns in 1907, in addition to what has already been mentioned.

Ruedi train depot, used as a tea room in the 1930s.

Ruedi, elevation 7585 feet. On left is the ranch of Mr. & Mrs. Will Henderson. Right center is Wm. Smith's home, hotel, and ranch, the Midland pump house, depot and water tank. Extreme right is the plaster mill with the schoolhouse left next to the hill.

Coy and Lila Ford, and their cute little blond children ("blonde" if it is a female) lived in the old Sam Phillips house close to the once existing plaster factory. It was Coy's job to walk the power line (as an inspector) from Thomasville to Sloss. Later, he was given the Hagerman Pass route which he patrolled on a snowcat. Both Bill Eppley and Fred Elmont went to school in Ruedi. Bill went there for three years before moving to Basalt. He lived on Smith Creek at the time with his grandpa Bill Gray. Fred Elmont says his teacher, for the one year he attended there, was Mrs. Ione Meredith. He loved to greet her each time he saw her in years after that. He lived with his uncle, Leon "Red" Nelson, on the Nelson Ranch. Mrs. Leon Nelson tells, elsewhere in this book, the pain and anguish they suffered having to leave their home of a lifetime on that ranch to make way for the dam and reservoir.

Rocky Fork Creek comes down west and south of Ruedi Dam. A work of nature is visible to someone with an imaginative eye —an actual huge stone fork with at least two and, perhaps, three tines. That must be where the little spot got its name. Before the dam was built, there was a cute little campground at Ruedi just about where the south end of the dam exists today. It had a few small picnic tables, one water tap and some wonderful shade from the big pine trees. We all hated to see that little spot go, but surely campgrounds like Little Maude to the north are far superior today.

Ruedi Lakes, John Ruedi Ranch, Smith Hotel.

It could get really cold in Ruedi in the old days. As hard as it may seem to believe, Bill Eppley reports that it was once sixty degrees below zero at Ruedi one winter in the thirties. Cliff Elmont also verifies that, having heard it from his uncle Red Nelson. Jim Crowley says he walked through Ruedi one time when an old man said to him…."Rather chilly today!" It was forty degrees below zero on that occasion.

A time or two, in the last couple of years, people have been discouraged from camping at the Ruedi Campgrounds due to the foraging of hungry bears. The terrible drought suffered in the area caused the normal food supply of wild animals to diminish. In Meredith and in other locations the bears came into town looking for food. Local newspapers reported that raptors began to suffer and that even fish were struggling to maintain an adequate habitat. Speaking of bears, south of Ruedi Reservoir about midway up the lake are two gulleys named East and West Thode. Fred Elmont and his cousins Ruth and Alice Elmont climbed to the top of them often. One day at the top of one of the Thodes they saw fresh evidence of a bear and hurried down as fast as their legs would carry them. The bears must love the altitude around

John Ruedi Ranch with the lakes in the background.

Ruedi and Meredith. One man in Meredith had to run a sow and her three cubs off in the middle of the night with a shotgun "persuader." He strongly felt the mother was after his dog for a meal. That was in the summer of 2001.

The Ruedi Dam has been guarded night and day in this day and age by several security guards hired by the federal government in light of the terrorist actions in our nation. Mr. Jimmy Olsen is the guard that I personally met one day. He was wearing a badge, had binoculars and a bullhorn, and a faithful German Shepherd dog named Bella. Mr. Olsen warned anyone coming suspiciously close to the dam to back away with their boats. He worked for the Smith Law Office who hired out to the government. He came from Cheyenne Wyoming. When he was not out there watching, someone else was. Though we feel secure about the safety of the dam

A security agent guards the Ruedi Dam.

under such protection, it is said that Basalt residents would have about a 40-minute warning should the dam ever be breached. Closer proximity to the dam would provide less warning in case of emergency. I am sure Mr. Olsen had access to a weapon had he ever needed it. Speaking of security guards... "Better safe than sorry!"

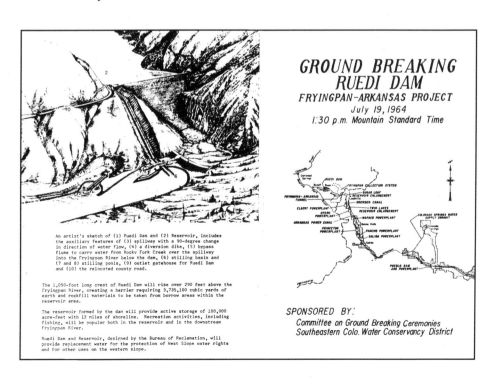

An artist's sketch of (1) Ruedi Dam and (2) Reservoir, includes the auxiliary features of (3) spillway with a 90-degree change in direction of water flow, (4) a diversion dike, (5) bypass flume to carry water from Rocky Fork Creek over the spillway into the Fryingpan River below the dam, (6) stilling basin and (7 and 8) stilling pools, (9) outlet gatehouse for Ruedi Dam and (10) the relocated county road.

The 1,050-foot long crest of Ruedi Dam will rise over 290 feet above the Fryingpan River, creating a barrier requiring 3,735,100 cubic yards of earth and rockfill materials to be taken from borrow areas within the reservoir area.

The reservoir formed by the dam will provide active storage of 100,000 acre-feet with 12 miles of shoreline. Recreation activities, including fishing, will be popular both in the reservoir and in the downstream Fryingpan River.

Ruedi Dam and Reservoir, designed by the Bureau of Reclamation, will provide replacement water for the protection of West Slope water rights and for other uses on the western slope.

GROUND BREAKING RUEDI DAM
FRYINGPAN-ARKANSAS PROJECT
July 19, 1964
1:30 p.m. Mountain Standard Time

SPONSORED BY:
Committee on Ground Breaking Ceremonies
Southeastern Colo. Water Conservancy District

Smith Creek

Smith Creek is the first stream east of Ruedi. Bill Eppley lived with his parents, Byrd and Olive Eppley, on Smith Creek before he moved to Basalt at about age eleven. He attended the first three grades at the little school in Ruedi. Tommy Neal went to school with him. Bill Gray was Bill Eppley's grandfather. Bill's daughter Olive married Byrd Eppley. Bill Gray was one of the early settlers on the Frying Pan. My good friend, Grace (Mrs. Harold) Silverstein of Basalt, was Olive Eppley's aunt and a sister to Bill Gray. Whenever Bill Eppley got into a fight near the swinging bridge, his mother had heard about it by the time Bill got home. Grace would get on the phone and tell Olive.

Frank Neal on the old Link Homestead at Smith Creek.

Bill was often in fights and was forever the protector of the "underdog." There was always a certain bully picking on Ronnie Bogue. Bill defended Ronnie. Another bully taunted Bill Eppley, himself. Miracle of miracles, that bully's father taught Bill how to defend himself and the bullying came to a swift halt one day. Hurray for heroes that fight for underdogs! Hurray for fathers who take sides with the opponents of their own bully sons! Down with big bad bullies!

The Eppleys and the Grays shared a tiny little "L-shaped" cabin on Smith Creek. It still sits there today. Little Bill slept by the pot-bellied stove in the larger part of the "L". So did his grandfather. His parents slept in the smaller part where they had a modicum of privacy. They drank the water right out of Smith Creek. Ugh!. The creek ran all year long. It was cold enough most of the year to run right through their ice box out in the ditch and keep their dairy products cool. They had no fear of giardia whatsoever, or any other water-borne disease. Bill did say they had to check now and then to make sure no deer had died in the water upstream. The Eppleys' little cabin sits just north of the Aspen Yacht Club Marina. Bill Eppley, as an adult, built that marina. He has always been handy with a Caterpillar and, in this manner, has made his living running heavy duty equipment in Colorado, Utah and Arizona. He resides in Salt Lake City today, as does the author.

North of the road, up Smith Creek, Byrd Eppley raised potatoes. Many thought it could not be done at such an altitude and with such a short growing season. Later he proved that wheat could be grown successfully at what we call

Frank Neal (left), Peg Meredith (standing), and Albert Carpenter (kneeling).

today "Ruedi Shores", above the former McLaughlin Lodge near Little Maude Campground.

When the Eppleys decided to move to Basalt, they bought Ray Jones' property up on the north hill and also his dairy cows. They took over the whole dairy operation. Young Bill helped to deliver milk and cottage cheese all over town. It was Ray Jones' other job to walk the power line from El Jebel to Sloss. Jenny Jones was Dutch and still spoke the language fluently. She was as short as Ray was tall. They were a nice version of "Mutt and Jeff." Jones, however, is an Irish name. My brother Fred used to like to ring Jenny Jones' doorbell just to ask her what time it was. She would go back into the house and return giving the exact time in Dutch. My, how Fred got a kick out of that! That was when they owned a nice home on Main Street.

The Eppleys turned a big barn on their hillside property into an ice house. The river at Ruedi, were Bill Gray owned additional property, made a big horseshoe bend. It also created a few ponds nearby. Gray owned those ponds and cut ice blocks from them in the winter time. He hauled them by wagon to Eppley's ice house in Basalt. I remember peeking in the old barn as a kid and marveling that the ice was still frozen in amongst the sawdust in mid July. A Mr. Smith, from whom Bill Gray purchased the land, was the original property owner on Smith Creek. Today, a family named Michaels owns the little cabin and the land. Bill says he made the little lake at North Fork adjacent to the old John Irions place.

Bill Gray, along with the Eppleys, maintained an old Essex car in their barn on Smith Creek. It was very hard to start in that kind of cold weather. You

John Irion's old barn at North Fork.

and I can hardly believe what they had to go through to start the car. They first heated the oil, which had been drained from the car, on a stove in the barn. Then they built a fire under the car heating the whole engine and framework. Then they poured the warm oil back in and gave the engine a crank. That is the only way they could get it started. (And we think we have occasional trouble with our autos?)

Eppley is a German name. They and the Grays and Grace Silverstein were all Seventh Day Adventists. The survivors still are today. Harold Silverstein, however, was possibly the only Jew in all of Basalt. I clearly remember hearing his bedtime prayers as I was in the nearby living room chatting with Grace. "Hear, O Israel, the Lord, our God, is one God!"

The Silversteins had a very spoiled and pampered Siamese cat. It was called Chiang-Kai-Shek. It had to sleep on top of the warm fireplace mantle to simulate the Mohave Desert where it was born. It ate the finest sirloin and crab meat. It dutifully went potty in the shower. It had been stroked and petted so much that its fur on the underbelly dragged the floor. Some children never got the care that cat got.

When Bill was a teenager in Basalt, he often pushed over Ray Jones' outhouse at Halloween. We asked him if the oft-told tale was true that he and a friend had taken a full load of salt and bacon rind from Ray Jones' shotgun right in the "derriere." Bill said the story was very true! He also used to delight in shoving Uncle Silvy's outhouse over down at the cabins by the swinging bridge. All the kids in town swore that Silvy was "in" the toilet the second year it was shoved over. He waited there to catch the vandals "red-handed." Since the door was downward, he had to wait for help to extricate himself from his embarrassing predicament. Bill could hardly deny the last story, because the author was there to witness it. Bill took a fellow student by the neck in the boys' locker room in high school, shoved his head in the urinal and flushed it. I asked him why he would do such a mean thing. He said: "The guy was forever picking on Ronnie Bogue." There was no way Aunt Grace could phone and tell mama that time. She didn't see it.

Meredith

Professor Meredith, for whom the town was named, died in a huge powder blast. He is buried one-half mile east of the old town site. That places his body halfway between old Meredith and the new town site to the east. Much mining and logging went on at Meredith. That would explain the presence of the blasting powder. The Biglows and Mr. Robert Reed joined forces with Gus Dearhamer and built a sawmill on Miller Creek. Today it is a favorite rendezvous for snowmobilers. Eight mills on the Frying Pan turned out 100,000 feet of lumber daily! Mills existed at Meredith, Thomasville, Biglow, North Fork, Norrie and elsewhere. Meredith is also the spot where 24 elk

Fred G. Jakeman.

from Wyoming were released in March, 1915, to replace those that had been depleted in the previous 25 years. Some other early Meredith settlers were: Andersons (whose daughter taught the first school), Roberts (who had another sawmill on Miller Creek), "Humpy" Miller (for whom the creek is named), Paul Billow (my relative), Keifners, Takamans, A. J. (Gus) Dearhamer, Fred Williams, Fred G. Jakeman (my grandfather), Mr. Beard, Mr. Saunders, Mr.

The old Meredith auto bridge after it was shortened in 1956.

Buck, the Roberts, Mr. Miltanberger, the Gilstraps, the Mysers and the Watkins. The Meredith School was built in 1894 for Miss Anderson. Later teachers were Lulu Thompson, who became Mrs. Claude Crowley, Margaret McHugh and Minette Miller, undoubtedly a relative of "Humpy."

Grandfather, Forrest Newkirk, owned land on both sides of the river at Meredith. His property was best viewed just east of the current river bridge. One can still see a little field on the north where he had a small cabin. On the south side of the river he built a larger home all by himself. One of his other homes was moved farther east and belongs to Doc Leonard's grandchildren. The author once ate a scrumptious Thanksgiving dinner in that old larger home near the bridge. It is now gone. The old majestic oven from that home now sits in Doc Leonard's cabin. It still operates on wood or coal and cooks just fine. The gauge on the oven still works. Grandmother Lydia used to test that oven by dropping a bead of water on the lids. When the water sizzled just right, she knew the oven was ready to bake. Grandmother made delicious home-canned corn and bing cherries (not to mention her cinnamon rolls, pies and cakes). One fellow once said: "My wife cooks just like mother." The other one answered: "Mine cooks like mother used to try to cook." Another husband was quoting the Bible where Jesus was asked to turn stones into bread. A newlywed said his wife could do better than that: "She can turn bread into stones."

Mr. Paul Billow, a far cousin of the author, had the property in Meredith before Mr. Newkirk bought it. Paul's children were Herman Billow and his wife, Mae. Herman is buried in Minturn, Colorado, and his widow, Mae, lives in Salt Lake City. Another cousin of the author was Fred Billow, son of Paul Billow. He was a brother to Herman. He and his wife, Charlotte, later lived in Ogden, Utah. When Fred and Charlotte still lived in Meredith, they owned a gasoline operated washing machine. Doubting a little that such a machine ever existed, the upstart incredulous author asked for verification. None other than the auspicious Jim Crowley says that they used to own one too. I wonder what other great inventions I missed out on? One day Charlotte was washing clothes. She got her long hair too close to the ringers. Sure enough, her hair was pulled in clear to the scalp. She managed to shut the machine off, but could not get herself free until Fred came home that night and rescued her. What a story!

The old Dearhamer Store sat due east of the current Meredith campground restrooms right by the lake. The original owners were August "Gus" Dearhamer and his wife Edith. They had a couple of large sheds near the store. The first store was actually a mere extension on the side of their home. Gus' children were Howard and Norma Deerhamer. Howard and his wife, Bobbie, later operated a nicer store. A lot of "craps" and card games were played in the store, especially when Howard ran it. He hated to lose and occasionally got quite irritated. He was single in his card playing days. Bobbie must have toned him down somewhat.

The old Dearhamer store moved a mile.

Gus bought vinegar in 25-gallon wooden barrels. Edith had to siphon it out with a rubber hose into smaller bottles for sale. One time all the bottles were full but she still had a mouthful of vinegar. She hated to waste it, valuable commodity that it was, so she spit it into an empty bottle and corked it for later sale. This is reported by an eye-witness who is still alive. The same eyewitness reports that Edith always placed a fairly heavy piece of Denver Post on the meat scale before weighing the meat "in order to keep the meat clean."

Closer to Meredith than to Ruedi was the old yellow two-story Williams home. It was across the river on the south side approximately two blocks from the Dearhamer Store. It was approached by a narrow footbridge over the water. The house must have had beautiful hardwood floors. When it was demolished to make way for Ruedi Reservoir, the floors were carefully removed and placed in Marie Bowman's home at Seven Castles. My brother, Cliff, helped to remove those floors. I believe the house was burned. Al Garnier and his family once lived in there. I used to go to school with his two daughters. I will not mention their names due to an embarrassing mishap they had on that little bridge one day. It had been raining quite hard. The Basalt school bus sat on the highway honking for the two girls to hurry. In their rush they both slipped on the wet bridge and plunged right into the river.

The very first school bus on the Frying Pan, that anyone knows of, was run by George McLaren. If you did not know George, you really missed out on a piece of "Americana." There may have been one earlier unknown driver before

George McLaren and percheron team with two hand cars and long racks with several tons of spuds in the spring of 1919. Note the braking poles with ropes for downgrades.

George. George had a one-and-a-half ton cattle truck with side racks and a canvas stretched over them to keep the kids dry. They entered the truck with the help of a ladder. Imagine that! How much like cattle they must have felt. Later, McLaren owned a smaller truck with a green wooden box on the back entered by a small back door with one glass pane in it. The author remembers this bus well. It probably held eight kids at most, and ten in a tight squeeze. The only heat was what happened to filter in from a small window between the driver and the back end.

Dale Nyberg, a passenger on the bus and son of Joe and Nellie Nyberg, affectionately called the bus the "hog crate." Dale was from Thomasville and was one of the best basketball players Basalt ever had. He had a handsome older brother named Harry. Dale was short compared to some of the players and we used to claim he could cut under a taller opponent's legs and score before anyone realized it. He was a cousin to Wyland Kittle. Nellie Nyberg was a daughter of Fred and Ethel Williams. She and her sister, Jessie Kittle, were the only girls in a family of ten or more children. Some of the more well-known boys were Gene, Bud (Leroy), Bob and Troy.

Another famous passenger on the bus was an easterner, Catherine "Kitty" McLaughlin. Her father owned the Diamond G Guest Ranch where the Ruedi Campgrounds are now. The area used to be known as Dry Gulch. I believe my twin cousins, Ruth and Alice Vagneur, used to work up there for the McLaughlins. Fred McLaughlin was also a state legislator. One part of the current campground was named for my first cousin Maude Usel and her mother, also a Maude. Her husband Stanley Usel spent many years working for the Forest Service and so he had the privilege of naming part of the campgrounds. He named his part "Little Maude."

A couple of severe frosts killed a lot of the blossoms in the spring of 2001 and made the chokecherries and berries very scarce for the bears. Experiencing great hunger, they came down to towns, campgrounds and private homes looking for food. One night the next summer my brother, living at Meredith, experienced great commotion outside in the middle of the night. His dog was in a frenzy. A flashlight revealed a mother bear and three young cubs foraging around the trash can. She refused to leave. It was thought that she fully intended to eat the dog. Only a blast from a shotgun convinced her she had probably better "skeedaddle."

Little Maud (Maude) Campground at Ruedi, named for the author's aunt and his first cousin, Maude Usel of Fort Collins. Stanley Usel worked for the Forest Service summer after summer and got the privilege of naming it.

Thomasville

Calcium was the original little settlement east of the current town. As one passes the two remaining lime kilns he is in the center of old Calcium. The town had most of its houses east of the river bridge and at the foot of Devil's Chimney. There were four lime kilns at one time, but now only two remain.

The two surviving lime kilns at Thomasville in 1938. The kilns were closed in 1910, reopened in 1938.

First called Calcium, the town later moved west and became Thomasville. It was called Calcium in 1888 when the Calcium Limestone Company formed there. It was one of the very first towns ever on the upper Frying Pan. The kilns were later bought and operated by the Colorado Lime and Fluxing Company. They produced powdered lime for use in smelting metal ores.

Calcium was absorbed by Thomasville in 1890. Just as Calcium switched to Thomasville, other stations along the way experienced name changes too. Quinn's Spur became Biglow. Muckawanago became Orsen. Sloane became Sloss. Wilson's Quarries became Peach Blow. And, finally, Aspen Junction became Basalt. Thomasville was named for a Mr. Thomas who engaged in mining and smelting in the area. He had a mountain named for him on the north side of town and he also had his own smelter on the north side of the river. A siding (spur) took off from below Devil's Chimney, crossing Lime Creek and sneaking along the mountainside until reaching north Thomasville about a mile-and-a-half later. Mr. Thomas processed ore from the Bessie Mine on Porphyry Mountain and from others near the Lime Creek–Divide Creek areas. When the mines near Divide Creek played out, someone "salted" them with fool's gold and sold them to a gullible investor. When the Bessie Mine also played out, the smelting business came to a halt in Thomasville for good.

Thomasville once had a boarding house, a hotel, a restaurant, two saloons and many log houses. Most houses were on the south side of the stream and to the east. Richard Neal's grandmother once lived in the old Calcium Saloon. Further west, by the depot, was the old Buckhorn Saloon. The old school is now the Methodist Church. It once sat down the hill further to the north from its current spot. The first post office ever on the Frying Pan was at Calcium (Thomasville). Nellie Daugherty ran the boarding house. She opened the first post office in it in March of 1888. She married my great uncle Charles V. Noble and he became

The old school, now a church.

postmaster for six years. Grandmother Newkirk (once a Jakeman and then a Nelson) tells a funny story about Charlie before he married. Grandma would bake enough baking powder biscuits for two meals—the evening meal and breakfast. Often she would awaken to find all the biscuits in the pantry gone. She suspected Charlie of eating them but could not prove it. One day at breakfast, when the biscuits were again missing, she announced that she hoped someone didn't die. "I put rat poison in the biscuits." Uncle Charlie (grandma's cousin) leaped up from the table and grabbed his throat yelling: "Help, I've been pizened!" The biscuits never disappeared again. Grandmother also had several Hennings relatives living in Thomasville.

The old John Irion's house at North Fork.

Later, the Thomasville post office moved to the Irions home. Those Irions really got around (North Fork, Thomasville and Basalt). I used to shop for groceries in Basalt for Mrs. Nel Irions in her old age, widow of John Irions. Their old home at North Fork has been remodeled several times and many of their old out buildings such as the barn still exist in dilapidated condition. Russel LaPree replaced Noble as postmaster and held the job for six years, running a store simultaneously.

In 1898, at the limestone kilns, a Mr. Breen pulled some hot powdered limestone out of the kilns with a long scraper. He got too close to a quantity of dynamite nearby. The hot scraper touched the powder and blew Mr. Breen to bits. It rattled the lime kilns causing mild damage and even shook the windows of George McLaren's home nearby. A small chute existed in front of the kilns to load the powdered lime into railroad cars for use at smelters elsewhere. It's too bad there wasn't an OSHA organization in those days to protect the health and safety of the workers.

Though Mr. Thomas ran the smelter in Thomasville, it was owned by the St. Louis and Colorado Smelting Co. As long as the smelter seemed to be a booming business, Mr. Lige Thompson enlarged his boarding house and it became the Thompson Hotel. He also ran a sawmill on Deadman Creek. At that time, and ever after, Thomasville was a bigger "burg" than Meredith ever was. In 1899 Uncle Charlie Noble reopened some of the lime kilns. The Bessie Mine attempted once again to produce ore (Swineford and Billow operated it). Paul Billow was a relative on my mother's side.

Though mother always said she was born at Thomasville, her homestead was really down the road about a half mile toward Meredith. It was on the north side of the river right next to Jakeman Creek, which was named for her father, Fred G. Jakeman. Every time my brother Cliff and I look at that spot, we are reminded of two things: how much we would like to clean out the mouth of Jakeman Creek so that it looks like a creek and how much we miss seeing mother's old house on the spot. Jim Crowley brought us much joy when he said that the old house had been taken apart and reassembled in Thomasville. It is the second house on the right as one is headed east. We felt extra joy to see rabbits frolicking in the front yard. We were told they were once tame but that now they roam wild as the original owner abandoned them.

Aauthor's mother's place of birth, moved from Meredith.

Nellie Noble, mother's maternal relative, once held a dance in her home in Thomasville. She and her Noble relatives (no pun intended) are all buried in the forgotten little cemetery on the south hill above Thomasville's east end. One stone marker still carries the name "John Noble." The Alhambra

Hall was the favorite dance place in town. A masquerade ball was held in it in 1899. After the ball Nellie Noble invited the whole crowd to her restaurant for supper. Who said they didn't know how to have fun in those days? Her restaurant may have been in one end of Thompson's Lodge. Whenever a new teacher came to town, such as the one who arrived once from Aspen, a special dance was always held to welcome her. I imagine the old cowboys and mine workers made darn sure they were in attendance to flirt with that new "school marm." Some of their descendants were still dancing the "one step" well into the twentieth century.

Hunters that worked for the railroad in Denver enjoying themselves at the Frank Neal ranch in Ruedi. 1935. The logs of the building came from John Ruedi's original home.

Fred G. Jakeman was from Blue Grass, Iowa, near Davenport. He homesteaded between Meredith and Thomasville early enough in the eighteenth century to qualify the entire family as Colorado "pioneers." His wife, Lydia, our maternal grandmother, was from Olwein, Iowa, north of Des Moines. How they ever met in the Wild West is beyond me, but meet they did. After they married they had mom in 1897, Maude in 1899 and Fred G., Jr. in 1901. Then Grandpa Jakeman was killed. We kids were told it was from an appendicitis attack but, when we were older, the real truth came out. He was murdered when he beat out an opponent in a political race. The day after the election the rival came to his front door and shot him point blank. He died on the train on the way to Aspen.

Later, grandmother married Swan M. Nelson, who logged at Norrie and later helped her ranch at Ruedi. He was the father of four boys: Frank, Albert, Leon ("Red") and Earl. How they all crowded into one small home in Norrie later owned by a Miss Elliott of Glenwood, plus boarders, I will never know. It is reported that Swan Nelson tried to sell the ranch at Ruedi out from under grandmother, so she had to give him his "walking papers." The ranch was then run by her sons. Much later in life she married the former railroader, Forrest D. Newkirk. To us she was always Grandma Newkirk. She moved to Basalt with Mr. Newkirk, after having lived with him at Meredith. For years she single-handedly kept the Methodist Church afloat financially by her selling of greeting cards and her making of rag rugs. It is a coveted thing in the family to still have one of her rag rugs or one of her famous homemade patchwork quilts. I still have two.

The firehouse at Thomasville, home of Doc Leonard's famous annual fish fries.

Today, in Thomasville, the notorious cowboy Jim Crowley owns a trailer where Nellie Nyberg used to live. The trailer sits today where the old Buckhorn Saloon used to sit. Next to the saloon was Lige Thompson's old boarding house, later to become a hotel. He was also the Justice of the Peace at the time (around the turn of the century). Nellie was a daughter in the famous Williams family known all over the Frying Pan. There were eight boys and two girls. The other girl was Mrs. Eldon Kittle of Carbondale. Nellie and Joe had two hand-some boys, Harry and Dale. I think both boys served in the military and Dale was famous as a good basketball player at Basalt High School. He and Harry both rode in the famous old George McLaren school bus which Dale once affectionately named "the Hog Crate." Dale was one of the shorter ball players and we used to joke that he could run under the opponent's legs and score before the opponent knew what happened. Handsome Harry married one of the pretty Basalt girls.

After Joe and Nellie separated, Joe would come into the Basalt Sundry where I worked and order from our soda fountain. His favorite order was a bowl of chili with a side of potato chips. He would carefully remove his false teeth and place them on a napkin on the counter. When his hot chili would arrive, he would place the potato chips in it which instantly turned them to "leather." Then he would sit there and gum his food, which usually took him about half an hour. We always loved him and felt sorry for him. We likewise loved Nellie and her two boys. Joe used to harvest timber at what we later called the Diamond J Guest Ranch. He snagged the logs out with horses.

Nellie Nyberg was a very warm and loving person. She used to work in a café in Thomasville. She died before the thing blew sky high one night in a terrific natural gas explosion. That ruined a bar and café and a two-story motel which burned to the ground. You should have seen the shocked look on certain faces that used to frequent the place when they rode up and saw it utterly devastated. I felt sorry for the owner who was a cordial man. If his café was closed for the day, he would signal through the window to go into the bar and "I will feed you there." I watched a drunk fall off the bar once while we were eating nearby. He prided himself in falling all the way to the floor without spilling a precious drop of his beer. While we were eating, an old dog wandered in and started eating morsels off the floor. As the waitress arrived ("bar Miss") to take our order, we all swore she was wearing only a fancy slip. My older brother Fred swore she was flirting with him as she took our order. I told him later that it was one of the wildest places in which I had ever eaten. It was not so on the closed restaurant side. It was not so when Nellie Nyberg worked there.

Jim Crowley helped each of his children build a beautiful peeled log home at Thomasville right on the river bank. His daughter Lea and her husband John Vasten, my old high school buddy, have a home east of the other two. One cannot miss these beautiful homes as he passes through Thomasville. West of Lea's is one belonging to Frankie. Then the next one west belongs to Jimmy, Jr. We don't know why Betty doesn't have one there too, making the foursome complete, but she doesn't. She does have a nice home near Silt, Colorado, however. That must be what attracted Jim Crowley, Sr. down to the Rifle area fifteen years ago—the warmer "southern" climes with their milder winters. You're softening up, cowboy Jim! Or was it that good-looking girlfriend, Lila, that drew you there?

On the north side of Thomasville is Nelson Gulch. An old man, Mr. Nelson, lived up the gulch in a two-story log house. He lost his wife and became very despondent. One night he sat on his bed getting ready to sleep and

The Crowleys. Top, left to right: Frankie Straight, Lea Vasten, Jim Crowley, Sr., Betty Ortell, Jim Crowley, Jr.

suffered a heart attack. When he didn't appear in town the next day, people went searching for him. There he was frozen stiff, still sitting upright on his bed. The train always carried bodies to the nearest mortuary. As the body lay frozen in the Thomasville depot, someone tried to thaw it out so the legs would straighten. They put a heavy door on the body. As the body thawed, the legs suddenly straightened moving the door abruptly. "Lige" Thompson, who was assigned to guard the body, nearly jumped through the station ceiling with fright.

Next to Nelson Gulch was Suicide Gulch. The old man who lived up there had a very fine team of horses. One day in the late 1800s he was told he had cancer and had a very short time to live. He tied his team to a tree near his place and shot them. Then he shot himself. In this manner the gulch obtained its name.

The Jakeman place between Meredith and Thomasville was bought by a Mr. Schmeider. Claude Crowley, father of Jim, bought it from Schmeider. Now it is owned by the Cap K Ranch. Before Mr. Schmeider (not Schneider) bought it, he met Joe Goddard attempting to cross his very private bridge. (The bridge is now long gone.) The two engaged in fisticuffs on the bridge. Old Joe sliced Mr. Schmeider's belly with a big knife. Schmeider, according to Jim Crowley (who got the story from his father who was there), chased Mr. Goddard toward Meredith.

Cody James Crowley, "The Little Buckaroo", Jim's grandson.

Crowley says that for years the story floated all around Meredith, whether true or not, that Schmeider "....killed a man and fed him to the hogs." Let us hope it was nothing more than a juicy rumor.

A lovely home in mid Thomasville today belongs to Mr. And Mrs. Richard Neal. I think the Neal story goes back a long way in the valley. The home has an unusual design which makes it not only unique, but attractive as well. It is well landscaped and has tomatoes growing out front. Early frost in the fall causes Mrs. Neal to have to cover her tomatoes. My brother Cliff also reports

Mr. and Mrs. Richard Neal's lovely self-built home at Thomasville. The Neals were an old standby name at Ruedi.

that while he was staying in Doc Leonard's old cabin once in Meredith, a one-inch deep hail storm blanketed Meredith in August. While staying at Aunt Linda's in Blue Lake near El Jebel one August as I researched this book, Aunt Linda said it felt like autumn in the air. What a short growing season Ivanhoe and Sellar and Nast must have had, not to mention Norrie, Thomasville and Meredith. Not too far from Richard Neal's self-constructed home is a pretty little home on the opposite side of the road that is built out of what I call "blond logs." Near it sat the old Calcium Saloon.

There is a move afoot to restore the two old kilns at old Calcium. I hope so. The cracks in them seem to be getting bigger. What a shame two other kilns are already long gone. One sat on the bank across the road from the two remaining ones. A cable ferried stone from the obvious quarry near where Lime Creek dumps into the "Pan" to a spot across the river where the missing kiln sat. A third one sat to the right of the remaining two right where a huge pine tree stands today. One can walk the river bank and see exactly where the fourth kiln sat by investigating rock deposits

The fourth large lime kiln at Thomasville. Now gone. 1965.

109

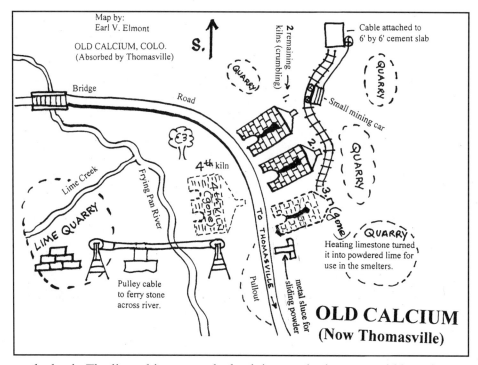

Map by:
Earl V. Elmont

OLD CALCIUM, COLO.
(Absorbed by Thomasville)

S.

2 remaining kilns (crumbling)

Cable attached to
6' by 6' cement slab

QUARRY

QUARRY

Bridge

Road

Small mining car

QUARRY

Lime Creek

Frying Pan River

4th kiln

4th kiln (gone)

QUARRY

2nd

3rd (gone)

LIME QUARRY

QUARRY

Heating limestone turned
it into powdered lime for
use in the smelters.

Pulley cable
to ferry stone
across river.

To THOMASVILLE

Pullout

metal sluce for
sliding powder

OLD CALCIUM
(Now Thomasville)

on the bank. The lime chips cover the bank in exactly the same width as the size of the old kiln. If one needs further help to find the spot, look directly across the road from the big tree still standing west of the existing kilns. What a sight that must have been to have seen stones coming across the river on a cable car! What a hotbed of activity old Calcium must have been! Grandmother's brother was also once the foreman at those lime kilns. His name was Lester Hennings. He died later in Corvalis, Oregon. He was also part-time sheriff of the area.

At the Thomasville depot, giant milk cans once sat containing 250,000 fingerling trout for Woods Lake. The depot was 14 feet by 36 feet. A section house for the workers was 24 feet by 30 feet with a 10 feet by 12 feet addition. There was also a bunkhouse and some stock pens. (The depot also had a "telegraphone", but we haven't figured out yet what that was.) Thomasville had a turntable and a dining car side track. Dining cars were added to the train there and dropped from it also for cleaning and re-stocking. This happened from 1907–1914. An agent operator was on duty at the depot from 7:30 a.m. to 7:30 p.m. The spur for the lime plant held 35 cars. In 1905, a total of 153 cars full of lime left Thomasville. Twelve cars left loaded with uncrushed lime rock. In addition, 210 cars of logs, 20 cars of cut lumber, 25 cars of hay, 7 cars of cattle and one car of potatoes sailed out of town.

The bulk lime rock and powdered lime were shipped to Leadville and were used as flux in the smelters. Sugar beet factories also used the lime. Lime was burned in the kilns to get pure lime powder. Another lime quarry at Newett on the eastern slope got all of the business eventually. It was the first stop east of Buena Vista. The Thomasville quarries were abandoned before WWI. They reopened briefly in 1938 but did not last long. All operations moved to Newett since freight charges were less on that side of the mountain.

The Thomasville Depot. (Right to left): Link Cass, Paul Billow, Bert Holder, Jim Pugh, Dan McDonald.

Why calcium and limestone were so important: We learn the following about calcium (CaO or Calcium Oxide) from *The Encyclopedia Americana*, vol. 17, 1999, page 487.

"It is also called quicklime or hydrated lime or hydraulic lime. It is one of the oldest chemicals ever used by man. It was used in Mesopotamia as mortar in 2500 B.C. The Romans used it for hydraulic cement which can set under water.

"In the middle ages it loosened hair from pelts and prepared skins for tanning.

"By Renaissance time it was used in farming to reduce soil acidity. It was used in glassmaking, papermaking and tanning. It was used for road bases, airport runways and as a soil stabilizer. It was used in Portland Cement. It is still used in masonry mortar and in plaster. It is also used with wet sand to make sand-lime brick.

"It is used as a basic flux (washing) in producing iron and steel. It dissolves impurities out of both.

"Lime takes magnesium out of seawater.

"Dead-burn lime lines the interior of lime kilns and furnaces.

"Lime treats water and is used as a water softener. Lime helps kill bacteria in water.

"It helps control acidity in the treatment of sewage. It helps keep boilers clean.

"It can be white, gray or yellow. It has a musky odor.

"The melting point of quicklime is 4,676° Fahrenheit. The boiling point is 5,162° Fahrenheit. It becomes luminescent at high temperatures. It was used to light theatrical stages and was called "limelight." A saying was born ever since. "He enjoys so much the limelight."

The top view of one of the lime kilns at Thomasville showing where the bulk rock went in at the top to be cooked into powdered lime.

"When wet, it can neutralize hydrochloric, nitric and sulphuric acid.

"488 btu's of heat are released per pound.

"Slaked or hydrated lime comes as a putty or as a dry powder.

"American quicklime is purer than that of South America or Europe. It is 88-94% pure calcium oxide.

"If you heat it too hot, it is "dead-burned." It loses its porosity.

"It is also used in luminous paint."

Devil's Chimney and Woods Lake

Less than a mile above Thomasville on the north side of the road is the cute little oddity of nature known as the Devil's Chimney. It stands as a sentinel above the Eagle Road to Woods Lake. It is a photographer's delight. If one passes the two old lime kilns above Thomasville and then the river bridge, he will see the Devil's Chimney high on the mountain to the left. The giant stone monolith has a large opening in the bottom and is hollow clear to the top. If one lights a fire in the bottom (which we do not recommend), smoke will come out the top. In 1963, when my wife Claire and I were newlyweds, we did such a thing. To our great delight huge clouds of billowy white smoke came out the top when we lit a few pages of newspaper. With the summer droughts as bad as they have been for years now, we wouldn't dare try that.

At the base of Devil's Chimney is a large clearing among the trees that looks like it would make an excellent campground. It is close to the bridge on the left just out of Thomasville. A CCC Camp once sat there. These camps were an attempt by the federal government to put people back to work after the terrible depression of the late twenties and early thirties. The initials stood for "Civilian Conservation Corps." They are the group that built the Chapman Dam above Norrie. My oldest brother, Bill, helped to build it. The camp at Thomasville boasted the following: 200 men in camp, one doctor and several cooks. Surely, there were also laundry personnel. Basalt had one of these camps too. It was once the old railroad hotel and now is the Primavera. The workers at

Devil's Chimney at Thomasville.

Devil's Chimney, or old Calcium, slept in white tents mounted on wooden platforms. In other areas these tent cities had cement platforms. This combination of wood and cloth seemed common all over the Frying Pan. Nast once used

The Colorado Midland Railroad bridge just east of the McLaren R anch near the mouth of Lime Creek. The rails and road at the bridge were torn up in 1920/1921.

similar accommodations for tourists seeking recreation and pleasure.

Further west from the chimney we always found our favorite mountain flower, the state flower, the Colorado blue and white Columbine. It seems to like to grow in shady areas with fairly moist soil. One time in another part of the Frying Pan we found a two- or three-acre field full of them. We had never seen so many when, usually, they grow sparsely and are rather hard to find.

To get to Woods Lake Resort, take a left turn while going east just beyond the Thomasville bridge. On the way up you will pass Devil's Chimney and a fish hatchery once operated by Clarence Bowles. The hatchery is still there. Next come the lovely meadows of Lime Park. Tourists loved to go to Woods Lake to fish and canoe and spend their honeymoons. Horseback riding was a favorite pastime. Retired people liked to spend their entire summer up there.

In the early 1890s Mr. Jim Woods, a Mr. Peisar and Peter Englebrecht started the little resort fed by Lime Creek. The lake was already there when these gentlemen arrived. They constructed a number of cabins and a lodge for their headquarters and for eating.

Eventually Peter Englebrecht got possession of the place and enlarged it. He ran it for two-and-a-half decades. Soon he built another lake nearby and established a post office, calling it Troutville. Eventually there were three lakes up there. There was also one semi-spectacular waterfall. After the Englebrechts, the owners were the Luthes. Next the place came to be owned by Delbert and Arthur Bowles. Delbert died and Arthur later sold it to the famous singer, John Denver, and his associates. What will become of Woods Lake now that the famous John Denver is gone?

In the first half of the twentieth century, it was young Phyllis Bowles' job to help cook and clean the resort. Her family needed twelve workers in the summertime to run the place. Phyllis' mother was Thelma Bowles. Young Phyllis Bowles married the love of her life, that dashing Johnny Hyrup of Basalt, son of the famous railroad worker and town marshal, Walt Hyrup. When first married they lived on the ranch owned by my first cousins Stanley and Maude Usel. The ranch has since been sold and sub-divided and is known as Holland Hills today. In an interview with the Johnny Hyrups at their lovely and spacious new ranch near Parachute, Colorado, the author was pleasantly surprised to hear Johnny call Phyllis "Ma." I'll bet he learned that from his illustrious pool-playing father, Walt. I envied the Hyrups in their peaceful and quiet ranch setting far away from noise and pollution. Phyllis complains that the coyotes are eating her cats. If that is their worst problem, we won't worry about them. Johnny and Phyllis celebrated their fiftieth wedding anniversary in the fall of 2002. People came from far and wide to pay their respects.

Johnny spent most of his life in heavy duty construction and more than once he rearranged the topography on the Frying Pan. He still has enough machinery parked in east Basalt, the sale of which would ransom a king. Johnny is a first cousin to the wonderful Patricia Hyrup Yale of Buena Vista, Colorado. They share in common a famous grandfather, Jens Peter Hyrup, the first in the family to ever come to Basalt. He was from Denmark as we have mentioned elsewhere. He and his wife are buried in Basalt.

Beaver dams on Lime Creek about a mile above the Frying Pan road on the way to Woods Lake.

Diamond J

The Diamond J Ranch was originally Muckawanago. Muckawanago was just before one reached Biglow (the North Fork turnoff) on the way east. It was an Indian word meaning "The place where the bear walks." I believe Len Shoemaker said in his book that he often saw one at that spot. Like the railroad people often tended to do, they changed the historic name Muckawanago to Orsen's Siding. This area was also noted for logging. It seems like the entire upper Frying Pan was one giant logging operation. Harvey Biglow and his ever-present partner, Robert Reed, were the first two to ever start logging operations at Muckawanago. A large timber mill existed right on the spot. Later, the logging operation was moved up to Biglow. Biglow and Reed also ran a logging operation at Meredith in partnership with A. J. Dearhamer on Miller Creek.

Though one book claimed the big beer parties were held at Muckawanago, Jim Crowley says: "No Way!" He and his father, long time residents, say the beer drinking and picnics and merry-making were further up the road at Nast. They claim Muckawanago has always been a quiet peaceful place.

Muckawanago was first developed by the Biglows and the Bowles brothers. Later, Bruce and Alice Riley made a guest resort or dude ranch out of the place. On the property they held rodeos and horseback riding. They had Indian teepees and two fish ponds fed by Muckawanago Creek. They called it the Diamond J Guest Ranch. The Rileys were such friendly personable people. When they sold the guest ranch, they lived in a cute little house above Blair. At the Basalt Sundry, we always welcomed the ever-present smile of Bruce and Alice Riley. Lee Hendricks, of Basalt, says his whole extended family stayed at

the Diamond J for only $100 per day just two years ago. He seemed to think that was a great bargain. It appears that the enterprise is closed down today. Perhaps some new entrepreneur will come along and open it up again.

The barn at the Diamond J Ranch built by the Bowles family in the 1930s.

Biglow

A small railroad siding was usually called a "spur." Harvey Biglow had one at his place for loading logs. It was first called Quinn's Spur. One of the best spots for seeing evidence of an old spur is below Mallon Tunnel on the south side of the road and slightly over the cliff. It is above Sellar. If one drives slowly, and has a passenger on the right side watching, one can spy the old railroad ties still decaying in place. At Quinn's Spur, or Biglow, they unloaded a steam engine and all the machinery for a saw mill. They called it the old Pratt Mill and it was due north of Biglow Resort. The mill was over a small hill on what they called Montgomery Flats. They cut lumber from there all the way over to Lime Creek on the west. An old Midland pond and ice house still exist at Biglow.

They held exciting dances in the old Biglow Lodge, which still stands along with its several cabins. The lodge stands north of Harvey and May Biglow's personal cabin called "Skunk Haus", where the Biglow children Keith, Maxine, Josephine, Burns and Dick were raised. Can you believe that May Biglow still had time to be one of the directors of Norrie School? The orchestra for the dances was led by Sister McKew and her brother. She played

Engine 305 at Biglow on the bridge over the North Fork.

the violin and he wailed on the saxophone. They also had a drummer. With 185 people nearby at Norrie, the dances were probably well attended. There is a large lovely new home further north on the property today. It is owned by John and Marge Swamley.

Biglow had its own electricity before many other places did. To keep things in perspective and to show what an extraordinary feat that really was, consider that Basalt did not have electricity until the 1940s. I always thought it was baffling that Utah had Colorado Telluride power in that state before we had

The old lodge at Biglow.

it right across the mountains in Colorado. Figure that one out if you can! How well I remember the old coal oil lamps and the black window shades. We had to blow the lamps out and pull down the window shades every time the city sounded its air-raid siren. That old hand-cranked siren warned us of flyovers. We never knew whose plane it was because the radar systems were either too poor or non-existent during WWII.

An old ditch at Biglow on the south edge of the property had a giant water wheel. The wheel produced power from the fall of the water. John Lumsden, brother-in-law to Harvey Biglow, and Frank Crowley, brother to Jim Crowley, built the apparatus. They had trouble in the winter time with the water freezing, so they insulated the ditch with planks and sawdust. What incredible "ingenuckity" for those early times!

Norrie

Norrie Colony and the Old Norrie School

Norrie never was laid out to be a town. Houses and businesses simply sprung up along a crooked dirt road. Norrie just happened! One legend says that Norrie was named for a notorious madam who plied her trade in that bustling men's town. However, there was a fairly high-ranking railroad man by that same last name. The reader must draw his own conclusions as to which is the correct source for the town's name. Most of the little communities in the early days were men's towns and Norrie was no exception. Norrie had several saloons and gambling, a fair amount of drinking and some fighting. Except for Basalt, Norrie was once the largest town on the Frying Pan with an excess of 185 people.

Norrie Colony as seen from the south mountain above it.

Norrie residents often used the Midland Railroad to get to Basalt. It was almost as quick to go to Leadville since it was only sixteen miles from the top of the Continental Divide. Surely, many a Norrie resident embarked on the famous wildflower excursions. The train was often their source for the procurement of supplies. Dozens of workers came in and out of Norrie to work in the logging industry. Above Norrie was Deadman's Gulch. From here much of the lumber was extracted. Giant log chutes helped to get the lumber down to the valley. At one time, Norrie had the largest lumber operation on the entire western slope of Colorado. Hundreds of thousands of board feet of lumber went out of there to the west and east. Though many timber supports for tunnels came out of Norrie, a lot of them came from mills immediately adjacent to the Hagerman Tunnel west entrance. The waste scraps still lie there in enormous piles blanching in the sun.

One of the very earliest settlers in Norrie was a Mr. Rufus M. Deeds. Due to his unusual manner of dress, he was referred to as "Squire Deeds." He loved to race horses. That seems fitting for a "squire." Frank E. Gowan started Norrie's impressive lumber business. One large single roof covered three buildings—the mill, the lumber yard and a store. The huge complex had a dance hall upstairs. Mr. Gowan was a lame man and had to ride sidesaddle on his horse. He opened a second lumber mill on the Frying Pan–Woody Creek Divide. He employed a total of seventy-five men

Norrie's distinctive ice ponds were there long before 1915 when my Aunt Maude, as a young girl, boated on the ponds with her good friend Eula Mitchell. In winter the ice was used by the Midland Railroad for its refrigerator cars. The cars had two doors on one side with a slightly elevated roof in the middle. A lid came off for dumping the ice in. Food was transported on both sides of the big ice bin. There was a huge ice shed in Norrie and others in Cardiff and Leadville. Basalt also had a huge ice barn, but its ice came from Ruedi via the Eppley family. The ponds in Norrie today seem to be only for fishing and for recreation.

Eventually, other owners took over the Norrie businesses. Aunt Maude always spoke of a Mr. Koch (sometimes spelled Kough) who came down from Aspen. The Biggs Kurtz Company of Grand Junction once owned Norrie Colony and, perhaps, still does. I have heard, though, that many of the eighteen homes or so are privately owned today. To the west of the colony, along the river, most of the homes are privately owned by people like the David LaMont family and his mother Betty, and the Clyde Vagneur family; also the Jamesons, the Mendicellis and the Whitbecks and perhaps others. I wish I knew about all of them.

Nearly ten years ago Aunt Maude pointed out to me that the foliage is immensely thicker in the Norrie area than when she was a child at the beginning of the twentieth century. No wonder! The largest lumber operation in western Colorado must have nearly denuded everything. She likewise reported that the old road came into town several feet south of the current road. If one sees huge boulders sitting west of the current entrance to Norrie, the old road ran right between those boulders. Many of the earlier buildings in Norrie were west of the current entrance gate.

Maude's home, last owned by a Ms. Elliott, a one-time Glenwood school teacher, sat close to the river on the right hand side of the road just before the bridge that leads over to south Norrie. In that old house Grandma Newkirk, who was then a Nelson, raised three Jakeman kids, four Nelson boys plus a husband and boarders. Did they sleep three to a bed sideways? How did she do it? And at the same time she was one of the directors of the Norrie School when Margaret McClure taught there (circa 1909).

My friend, Lee Hendricks of Basalt, now the current mailman for the Frying Pan, lived for eight years as a boy in Norrie. Lee goes early in the morning to the Basalt post office and bundles the individual mail for the families on the Pan. He is most efficient in his operations and comes dangerously close to each mail box without ever hitting one of them. Francis Johnson used to be the postmaster in Norrie. She gave it up and the post office moved to Biglow where May Biglow ran it. Strangely enough, it still kept the name of Norrie Post Office. Charley Tease was the postmaster much earlier in an old log house on the north hillside.

Lee Hendricks, Frying Pan mail deliver, poses with Emma Walling, the postmaster at Meredith.

Lee's father, Ray, was born in Aspen and his mother, Virginia, was born in Leadville. She was a sister to the famous Martha Waterman and her sister Mary, who recently produced their own little book called "Sis." Martha bought the old Pete Grange place near the current Holland Hills. Martha and her husband Leroy were business people in Aspen for years. They were among the best square dancers the Roaring Fork Valley ever knew, they and their in-laws, the Ray Hendricks. According to the Ray Hendricks family, who were the caretakers of the colony houses along with the Horace Hendricks and the Cactus Gold families, as late as the 1940s and 1950s the snow still used to get about eight feet deep in Norrie.

Norrie once had 50 log and frame houses. It boasted of a nice log school with five windows to each side and a nice frame addition added on to the east by John McLaren and his son George. The school was across the river and up a slight hill. The school was separated from the ball field by a wire fence with a nice turntable gate. The original part of the school held a large bell tower on top of the roof. The inside was kept warm by the usual potbelly stove. Occasionally the school teachers stoked their own fires. If the teacher was a lady, she could

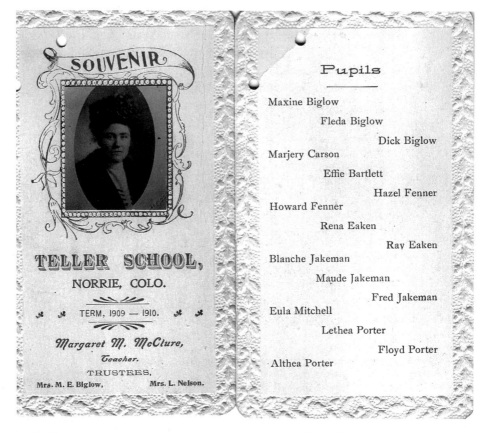

probably tap some burly male student to stoke the fires. Wood should have been no problem with a big mill nearby. Many flat wood pieces were available for shingles such as the log school had. Mother and her siblings walked less than a block to get to that school from their home. When mother had completed the senior grade in school, she became the custodian of the school.

Among the teachers named below that served in Norrie, Mrs. Margaret McClure is forgotten on the list. So I have reproduced an old program from 1909 with Mrs. McClure's pretty face on the cover. It lists all the students for that year inside. Notice Grandmother Nelson's name on the front cover. It appears that the directors were those who had the most kids in school. Among the teachers were a Mr. Rose (1896), Professor Rhodes, Ms. Skinner who later became Mrs. John McLaren, Ms. Brooks, May Epperson, Jewel Greener and Ms. Sanders; eight in all.

A lot of picnics and other social events were held at the school. It seemed to be in vogue for the ladies to wear a long white cotton dress. It was either a fashion trend for the times or a simple way to make a homemade dress out of white cotton. Though Jakemans and Nelsons attended that old school, it is doubtful that Leon and Earl Nelson got to finish there since their mother and father moved to a ranch at Ruedi. The Norrie School closed in 1918 when the railroad went out.

Later in this chapter the author will share interesting correspondence from siblings in Norrie while Maude Jakeman attended high school in Greeley. The letters give a wonderful cross-section of life in old Norrie back in those primitive and often difficult times.

Little Norrie Girl Attends School in Greeley

Imagine, back in 1915, attending HIGH SCHOOL in Greeley, Colorado, and then landing a teaching job in the public schools. Such happened to the wonderful Maude A. Jakeman, who later became an Elmont. She hopped on the Midland Train at age fifteen, with what must have been meager possessions, and made her way to Greeley. She graduated from high school with very high grades and accepted a teaching job in Byers and Deer Trail, Colorado. That is where she met her future husband, the dry farmer Herbert V. Elmont. With only those credentials she opened what she later called "the Elmont School." Later in life she came with her husband and children back to the area of her birth in Thomasville and to good old Basalt.

When my mother, Maude's older sister, went out to Byers for Maude's wedding, she met Herbert's younger widower brother, Paul. Mom fell in love with him and, three months later, was married by the same preacher in Denver that had married Maude and Herbert. We children have always thought it was special that

Four girls at Norrie in 1915. (left to right): Maude Jakeman, Eula Mitchell, Inez Matthews, Blanche Jakeman.

sisters married brothers. That made us "double cousins." Maude's twin daughter,s Ruth and Alice, repeated the "doubles duo" by marrying the Vagneur brothers of Woody Creek. Then the author's two daughters, Suzanne and Marilee, married the Davis brothers in Salt Lake City. Wow, a three generation habit! Later, my double cousins and I referred to ourselves as "kissin' cousins."

The great Dust Bowl of the late twenties and early thirties drove the Elmonts out of the plains. Most farmers went broke and the banks repossessed their lands. I have often wondered why they were not allowed to keep their lands. What good could they possibly do the banks? Herbert's journey alone to Basalt from the plains of Colorado is an epic story, indeed! There were very few paved roads in 1932. He traveled with a wagon loaded sky high with furniture and possessions, trailing some livestock behind. He went over high mountain passes and down into Eagle County. From there he went to Glenwood. The bridge over the Colorado must have had a cover on it in those days. Herbert had to rearrange his load to make it fit under the bridge. At night he slept out under the stars. What a story! When he arrived in Basalt, they stayed for a while with Maude's mother at Ruedi until a home opened up. Things were very tight at first economically. Maude found odd jobs where she could. Herbert grazed his milk cows along the roadways of Basalt.

One day a total stranger in a fancy can stopped Herbert along the road. He said he was a "Seitz" from Michigan and was looking for his Elmont relatives. Herbert replied: "I am one of them!" Herbert's mother, Barbara Ann Seitz Elmont, buried in Byers, was a sister to the man from Michigan, Alfred Seitz. What a small world! The father, Valentine Seitz, from Franklin, Pennsylvania, was once one of the richest men in Franklin. He invested most of it in the Bullion Oil Company which went broke. The fortune of Mr. Seitz disappeared overnight. I must tell you a funny thing about my "double cousin" Albert from Denver. He recently said: "I'm glad they didn't pass that 'Valentine' name onto me!" Albert's dad was Herbert Valentine Elmont. "Valentine" is a name from the heart of Europe. The British usually render it "Wellington", as in the famous Duke of Wellington who fought Napoleon.

The Sweet Little Lady with the Goats at Norrie

At Norrie lived Ms. Dorothy Claire Falk, known to her family and friends as "Aunt Cally." Cally was born in 1877 in Kansas City, Missouri. Her parents were Dieter and Wilhelmina Falk. Now there are two German names if ever I have heard any! My grandfather spoke German fluently, so I feel a kinship with Ms. Falk and her relative Mrs. Betty LaMont. Betty is a good friend of my friend, Mr. Jim Crowley. Betty is the mother of David LaMont, a U.S. postal worker in Basalt. I owe David the thanks for the use of his family photos of Aunty Cally in this book. Dorothy Claire Falk is buried in the Fairview Cemetery in Basalt. I am honored that her grave is immediately adjacent to my grandmother's. That seems only fitting. I am sure they chatted with one another while they both lived at Norrie. If Cally was there prior to 1920, she may have even chatted with my mother.

Ms. Falk had four sisters and one brother. The sisters were Bertha, Anne,

Francis and Gayle. The brother was Hobert. He was killed in a cycling accident in his early teens. Cally was raised and educated in Kansas City. As a young woman she became a nurse at a Kansas City tuberculin clinic. There she met and became engaged to the clinic's main doctor. Soon after, a terrible fire raged at the clinic. While busily helping to extract patients from the building, the doctor became entrapped and perished in the fire. This must have been a terrible blow to Cally. She later suffered what we would call today a nervous breakdown. It undoubtedly explains any possible "eccentricities" that one may have perceived in her later life. She left Kansas City and headed west.

Cally traveled through Colorado and ended up homesteading a small acreage now called "LaMont Pastures," which is above what is now Norrie Colony. There, with the help of Scott and Clarence Sawyer and others, she built a house, barn and two bunk houses. At the same time she began tending goats and raising hay. She had both Angora and milk goats in her herd which at times numbered as high as sixty goats. At that time goat's milk was thought to be highly beneficial to patients with tuberculosis, so it was shipped to a clinic in Glenwood Springs. Soon the sisters, all of whom had married, moved to Colorado as well. Bertha Pitcher and Anne LaMont became school teachers. Francis Vandeventer and her husband Lester were ranchers. Gayle Gaumnitz eventually ended up in California where her husband owned a dairy farm.

Aunt Cally spins goat hair into thread.

All were famous for their poker parties while living on the Frying Pan. They should have met Howard Dearhamer, who also loved to play poker, in his store,.

During the winter, the goats were moved to Basalt where they ended up on the train. They were shipped to either Golden or De Beque for the season. Both Grand Junction and Golden had tuberculin clinics which used the goat's milk. One knew the seasons were changing for sure whenever they saw Cally moving her goats upvalley in the spring and down again in the fall. Admittedly, she was a little eccentric, but at the same time a vital part of the colorful history of the Frying Pan. She reminds one of that other valiant shepherd of the "ovine"

A registered mills goat named "Granny" belonging to Dorothy Claire Falk.

family, Mrs. Georgina Terliamis, who walked her sheep from Basalt to Ivanhoe every springtime. There she leased grazing rights from the BLM.

Cally spent most of her life in Golden, Norrie and De Beque. Neighbors and her nephew, also called Hobert, helped to ease her loneliness. In 1946 the goat ranch was transferred to young Hobert, and Cally moved to Denver. There she died in 1949. Someday the author hopes to see a marker on her grave. How he wishes he had known her!

My oldest brother, Fred, seems to have known Betty LaMont's family well. Her maiden name was Swisher and she was born on property near Norrie known as the Swisher Resort. Betty's brother passed away while serving his country in WWII. The entry to the Swisher Resort, according to Fred, was the first road on the right past the Norrie Colony. Betty and David LaMont, we wish you well and consider ourselves privileged to know you.

A Glimpse at Life in Old Norrie (circa 1915)

Following is a series of letters sent to Maude Jakeman, while she attended her last years of high school in Greeley, Colorado. Such successful completion of schooling back then entitled her to teach in the public schools of Colorado with no further training. She established her first school in Byers, Colorado, on the eastern plains. As recounted earlier she met and married Herbert V. Elmont and her sister Blanche (the author's mother) met and later married Herbert's widower brother, Paul Elmont. When the famous Dust Bowl ended their farming careers on the plains, in 1932 they retreated to the former home of the women—Basalt and the Frying Pan Valley. Thus they came "full circle."

Lydia Jakeman.

The author felt these old letters give a better glimpse into life back then than anything else he could think of. He reproduces them here courtesy of Mrs. Alice Vagneur, of Holland Hills, who saved them when her mother Maude passed away in 2001. That makes these letters almost 90 years old. In the process the author learned what a wonderful sense of humor his grandmother Lydia Hennings Jakeman Nelson Newkirk had, of which the author had only the faintest knowledge.

Norrie, Colorado. March 28, 1916.

Dear Sister Maude:

How are you getting along in school? Have you got over your sickness yet? (Flu?) I have got the highest in my class. Kenneth Arnold and Lillie Lombardie don't read at all. They sit around and hear what I have to say and then repeat what I say.

We finally set the Christmas tree afire and burnt it all up. Blanche (18 yrs. old) is on the janitor's job at the school. Ruth Irions come to school today (from North Fork) and I guess she is trying to make up a whole year's grade. The land is just about all bare here and it is awfully muddy. We have another cat at home. It come from Irions. They have a whole family of "liddy" cats. That's what they call them after momma.

This is a very big letter for me, I think. We all have the measles and hope you the same.

From brother Albert (Nelson)

P.S. From brother Leon Nelson, "If you come home, I give you a kiss."

A humorous letter sent to Maude Jakeman's teacher at school in Greeley. The teacher was Mr. J. R. Bell. The date is March 21, 1915. The letter is from Maude's mother Mrs. Lydia Nelson in response to a letter from Mr. Bell indicating that Maude's grades were wonderful. (Intentionally misspelled):

Dere Sur: I got yhou leter saing that my girl Maud was expeld from skule. Naow I wont to no "y" she didn't cum hom to hur pore mammy. She rote me that she wuz broak and I recon the working is gude out yur way, and yu no the Proverbs, "the fule an his munny soon parrt, and az I sed befoar, (meanin the Proverb) What's the use? Walkin' is gude and times ar harder an apple juice, and our distrik skule is closed fur Skarlit fevir an r hens didn't lai many aigs naow dais an milk is scarcer un jak rabits an mai boy went ta hunt wesils and didn't git eny. Now weuns have no litle chiks. Have you' uns? An ma boy kilt a snow shu rabit and I rosted him and he wuz very gude ta et. And etcetera and etcetera, Jiminy crikits, i fergot ta menshun, aour rabit hed five young uns an thei all dide an the caow jumped in the pen with the kaf, an my old man bot anuther hoss, a kole blak an I thot it wuz a skare krow. Ha ha! I mus quit. Noose is scarce.

Yur fecconate frind from Pole Kat Korner an Koon Holler.

Jemima Hard Scrabble

1916. (From her mother, Lydia Nelson) Norrie, Colorado

My dear Maude:

Yours (letter) received and noted that you mentioned your old cat. In respect for your feelings, I am sorry to relate I try not to feel revenge to a dumb "beastie", but many times I would declare I would do a desperate deed.

Then a wee small voice would whisper: "Have you no sympathy for one who killed the mice and rats that ate your best bonnet?"

I thot she died of a broken heart. Papa (Swan Nelson) said she died of "beefitis." (Too much beef. She got into the pantry and ate all the roast beef.) Kind providence removed her. Tis well!

Ye brethren buried her in the barnyard with all the respect due a cat.

Your loving mama: (Lydia Hennings Jakeman Nelson .)

Norrie, Colorado.   Dec. 29, 1916.

Dear Sis: (Maude, half-sister in school in Greeley, Colorado)

How are you? I am fine and all are happy. I got your magic flashlight (a trick one). I was very happy to get it. You know I was in bed with Fred (an older Jakeman half-brother), and he said: "Look at my flashlight." So I looked at it and the snake came out and hit me in between the eyes. I got it Sunday morning. After while Fred give it to me. He said that you sent it to me but mean Fred kept it for a while. I scared Blanche with it and pappa scared her with it and she went to bed. (Angry) Leon (Nelson) and Earl (Nelson) were happy to get the toys (you sent). We had a nice program (at school). (Apparently Maude didn't get to come home for Christmas or she would have been present at the program.)

Joe Sawyer is working for pappa. Blanche is playing the Napoleon's last charge (on the piano). Well, it's nearly time to take care of the rabbits. Well, this is all I got to say.

From your brother, Frank (Nelson)

Norrie, Colorado. Nov. 28, 1915.

Dear Sister: (Maude)

I have received your letter and have been very glad. I have had four days off for Thanksgiving. We had turkey for dinner and we are going to have turkey for Christmas. Are you coming home for Christmas? I want you should be here for the dialogues (plays) at school. Blanche has been sick with the grippe.

Now I will tell you the names of the dialogues. There's "Daddy, Darwin's and Pappa's Christmas" and "Laurie's Christmas" and "Misses Trent" and I am "Chip" in Misses Trent. There's some other dialogues but I can't think of them. Well, this is not a long letter but this is all I can think of. (Over)

Yes, and old Joe Sawyer (hired hand) is back.

From your brother, Albert (Nelson)

P.S. I have shot four rabbits Saturday with my gun. I have a 22 Short-Long or Long Rifle. (He included a drawing of him on his horse.)

Norrie, Colorado. Jan. 23, 1916.

Dear Sis: (Maude)

How are you? I am fine. We are in school yet. You are coming home in June. I will be out the 19th of May. Pappa (Swan Nelson) is still hauling logs. He thinks he will be done in February. Well, Blanche is still home and broke her glasses. Mr. Mizer's nephew died Sunday morning at 2:30 a.m., Grace's baby.

Fred Jakeman (half brother) is getting some money from the county judge from the bank. I am not going on the ranch next summer. I am going with Dave's help to move camp. Mr. Dave Hargle is preaching up here. We have Sunday School. Well, this is all I got to say.

From your brother, Frank (Nelson)

(Postscript: Frank Nelson moved as a young man to Minturn, Colorado, to work in the metal mines of Gilman. He met a school teacher there, Mary Anderson, who had come from Aspen. They married. After Frank had several bouts with pneumonia, Frank's doctor told him to get out of the mines. He became a car salesman in Eagle, Colorado. He contracted another case of pneumonia and died. Shortly after, their only child, Gary, also died at about the age of two. Mary was heartbroken. When she left Minturn no one was aware of her whereabouts since. The other three Nelson boys lived much longer than Frank, one of them reaching the ripe old age of 93.)

Norrie, Colorado. Nov. 17, 1916 (Two days after Maude's birthday)

Dear sister Maude:

I suppose I have to answer all the letters. Pappa is sick and Frank and Fred got gum boots (rubber boots). And I didn't get any. But pappa went to the store and ordered a pair of them. Well, you better answer this letter. Ella, the teacher, said that if Fred (Jakeman) and Gordon (?) And Howard Benner didn't quit their meanness, she was going to expel them from school.

Are you coming home for Christmas? We are going to have lots of dialogues (plays) at school.

This is all I can say.

From your brother, Albert

(Fred Jakeman was the older half-brother to the Nelson boys. He, Blanche and Maude were the children of Lydia's first husband. Then she had four boys with Mr. Swan Nelson. When he left she ranched at Ruedi with the help of her boys. Later in life she married Mr. Forrest D. Newkirk and lived in Meredith and Basalt. Her son Leon Nelson continued ranching at Ruedi. Their old Norrie home was finally demolished by the Forest Service sometime in the 1970s.)

Nast To Ivanhoe Lake

Nast

Nast seems to have always been one or two private colonies. They were situated down the hill from the two giant railroad water tanks that sat right on Horseshoe Bend. We would expect a round water tank, but not the square one that sat right beside it, both fed from Ivanhoe Creek. There was a small railroad stop at Nast, not too much to brag about. If one had just alighted from the train or from a wagon or an automobile, he still had to walk or ride about a mile down into the "hollow" to reach the resort. Tiny facilities though they may have been, Nast was still considered a stop on the Midland. Today's owner is Mr. Miller. He calls his modern day operation the Frying Pan River Ranch. That is a nice name. He also owns property down river at Hopkin's Spur. He has a couple of alert and attentive caretakers watching both properties. Adjacent to his ranch and a little further east is a consortium of about eight owners who maintain another resort.

The lodge at Nast. It and its several cabins constitute the Frying Pan River Ranch.

Very much fun was had at Nast according to old-timers. And the greatest hostess on the whole Frying Pan lived there, Mrs. Hanthorne, the wife of Arthur Hanthorne the postmaster. Arthur was a partner to James Morris in running the resort. Certainly the dashing Mr. Morris, who owns the property today, is a descendant of the earlier Morris; it could not be coincidence. Mrs. Hanthorne was the most famous hostess that ever welcomed a guest at Nast. In the old photos the attractive hostess is either seen holding a bunch of wild flowers or a string of fish. She had both an attractive figure and face. She was usually photographed near some kind of small bowery.

Old-timers, and even one earlier book on the Frying Pan, tried to claim that the "wild" beer parties were held at Muckawanago, later to become Riley's Diamond J Guest Ranch. Not so, claims one eighty-six year old who says his parents were there! Ever since Robert Reed and Harvey Biglow founded a lumber company there, which later became Riley's place, it has been a tranquil get-away, a "dude ranch" if you will. The wild beer parties were held at Nast according to this old-timer from Thomasville. When people heard a party was to be held, they came all the way from Aspen and Leadville to join in the merriment. Swedes from the Leadville side brought their own kegs of beer on the train. Now we are not suggesting anything improper ever happened, just good old happy hours. There are only two suspect places for these occurrences, Nast and Riley's. This author votes for Nast!

The Nast Resort had its own little lake, a big lodge and private cabins which were often double occupancy. The first lodge was rather rustic. Much of the furniture in it and in the cabins looked homemade out of logs and sticks. Not so on the eastern slope where more of the money was. The hotels over there

A guest cabin at the Frying Pan River Ranch at Nast. Nearby is the Nast Colony, a separate private resort.

were grandiose and elegant. This is not to say the Nast lodge and cabins were not comfortable and enjoyable. They were! Today the lodge is replaced by a very nice and modernistic office and dining hall. It is obvious much work has been done on the place and Mr. Miller should be proud. No more are the walls and ceilings covered with boards and sticks. One day in the summer of 2002, as the author was walking around the property at Nast, he approached the small lake. There on the shores of that riparian paradise, the author found some of the most delicious wild raspberries he has ever tasted. My thanks to you, Mr. Miller. (I did not eat them all!)

The boiler of engine 301 which exploded on October 9, 1912, and is here shown being picked up about halfway between Nast and Sellar.

At least two major railroad disasters happened above Nast. The first was a runaway train from Sellar two miles above. The engineer was sure he had properly set the brakes on the engine. As he left it, the train began to roll downhill toward Nast. Faster and faster it went, crossing the two-hundred-foot trestle at rapid speed and thence heading down a much steeper slope. Miraculously, it passed the two water tanks at Nast without derailing. But it soon found the Horseshoe Bend to be too much for it and capsized on the south of the rail line into the rocks and trees and bushes. It lost all three cargoes of canned goods, coal and livestock. The cattle could not be saved. They all perished. The canned goods were smashed beyond use. Only the coal, with the most difficult of efforts, was salvaged. I'll bet heads rolled over that little incident. But then, can you blame a human for mechanical failure?

The second accident happened while the train was upward bound about a mile beyond the two water tanks. It seems inconceivable that a boiler would run dry just having passed not one water tank, but two. Perhaps there was a faulty gauge on the boiler. Whatever happened, one mile up the hill the boiler blew sky high, killing both the engineer and the fireman. There were bits of scrap metal everywhere. The engine that exploded above Nast was number 301. This tragic accident happened on Oct. 9, 1912.

In those days, things were always risky at best. When a wife and children bade an engineer farewell in the morning, there was never any certainty that they would see him again at the end of his shift. The same is true for the other workers on the railroad. One worker simply stuck his head out somewhere along the Frying Pan to check the weather. His head struck a bridge abutment, killing him instantly. Then there were all the runaway trains. If the brakes on the engine failed, workers had to run from car to car setting each individual hand brake. You will remember seeing in old movies the large metal wheels that had to be feverishly cranked like the wheels on the floodgate of some dam. If enough hand brakes were not set in time, the momentum and massive weight of the train caused it to derail at the first major curve. On some big curves a speed five or eight miles over that recommended could cause the train to derail.

An engineer on the Colorado Midland. 1915.

Some workers who died were buried right beside the tracks where the accident occurred. It was not always known where the worker came from nor what his address was. Often a terse telegram arrived, if the address was known, saying "We buried your kin beside the tracks where he died." Along this line, some people in eastern Basalt were digging one time to lay the foundations of a new house. They uncovered some human bones on that spot near the Ranger Station. A few were sure it was Indian bones. Others thought it was the remains of a railroad worker. Only God knows for sure.

Nast anciently had a post office. It opened on May 4th, 1909. Today, my good friend Lee Hendricks delivers the mail on the Frying Pan route and Nast is his last stop. Nast also had a ranger station where the author Len Shoemaker once lived and worked. He is the one that tells the story in one of his books about the mischievous hogs at Nast. A pair of large hogs was owned by the earlier Mr. Miller at Nast. They were always where they shouldn't have been and grazed all over creation. Mr. Shoemaker, grandfather of my good friend Leonard Shoemaker of Basalt, was stationed at the Nast Ranger Station in 1914. I am forever amazed at Mr. Shoemaker's memory of names, dates and places. His books are like encyclopedias for factual information.

The hogs were forever coming on Shoemaker's land and causing trouble. The big bore always seemed to want to fight. One day, Mr. Shoemaker was coming down the road lickety-split (in an auto, I assume) and there were the two hogs lying right in the road. Len spooked them so suddenly that the sow plunged right into the Frying Pan River at high water runoff time. He thought for sure she was a "goner" as she struggled to remain afloat. He was extremely worried about what he might say to Mr. Morris. Imagine his surprise when he awoke the next morning and found both the sow and the bore in his barnyard. He couldn't believe that she had made it out of the river. There she was suckling six little pink pigs. A couple of years later, Mr. Ed Koch (some say "Kough") was out hunting in the vicinity of Nast. He thought the bore was a wild one and shot it. He claimed that it attacked him. That was the end of one of the "runaway hogs" at Nast.

Sellar Meadow

At Sellar, two miles above Nast, is one of the prettiest meadows in the whole area. The author always expects to find deer and elk grazing there, but so far he has been disappointed. Mr. Jim Crowley said he saw some elk there once in autumn. This meadow is the gateway to some of the more enjoyable spots in the region such as Diemer and Sellar lakes. With Sellar as a departure point, the author once traveled to Diemer Lake. After thoroughly enjoying the lake and its environs, to our great delight we found the largest wild raspberries we had ever seen right at the outlet to the lake. We picked a half-gallon milk carton full of berries. We made pancake syrup out of them. The berries were as large as the thumb nail on an adult male. Jim Crowley claims that big meadow at Sellar is too swampy to have ever housed any homes. The train station, the meadow, a lake and other locations were named after a Mr. Sellar, a member of a famous banking family from England. He never dreamed that a brief stay in the area with a modest financial investment would bring him lasting fame.

On the north side of the tracks at Sellar was a huge coal trestle. It was not the largest on the route. The largest had a capacity of about 200 tons of coal. Sellar is home today to fifteen remaining charcoal ovens, albeit they are not in very good condition. The charcoal ovens at Sellar came along quite a bit later than the ones at Basalt. Sellar had fifteen and there were only half that many at Basalt.

Ruined charcoal ovens at Sellar above Nast. Fifteen ovens once stood here near a Midland Railroad siding big enough for 20 cars.

Charcoal, from wood, was easier to obtain before the plentiful coal deposits were found near Carbondale, Glenwood and New Castle. Both coke and charcoal were used in the smelters at Aspen, Cripple Creek, Pueblo and points in between. Coke burned cleaner and hotter in the train engines and was preferred to coal, especially when traversing smoky tunnels. In Basalt the local piñon pine went in one side of the ovens and came out the other as a finished product. Undoubtedly the same was true at Sellar. Making charcoal provided a good job for any man willing to tackle it. The author borrowed one old smoked-up Sellar brick from the charcoal ovens in hopes of putting it in a museum some day in Basalt. There is one man in Basalt that has enough old relics and souvenirs to fully stock a museum. He has his garage full of them. What a shame it would be if a house fire destroyed them forever. Hopefully some well-endowed man or woman will come along and help fund a museum.

Some of the deepest piles of cinders along the old rail line are on the upward approaches to Sellar. This testifies both to how busy the area was and to the steepness of the grade. Some of the cinders were thrown fifty feet from the track and straight uphill. A giant "wye" branching off to the right of the tracks headed east. The easternmost leg of the wye was long enough to accommodate twenty parked railroad cars between the main line and the coke ovens. How exciting it would be to go back to those days and watch the many industrious men with their sweaty, grimy faces. Likewise it would have been fun to watch the powerful engines pull their heavy loads up the steep grades, tooting their whistles all the while as they crossed the many impressive wooden trestles. Picture us all, perhaps, on a wildflower excursion. Some of the old-time women probably could have named every wildflower on the Frying Pan. Further, picture us stopping at Hell Gate for a breathtaking view at the deep chasm hundreds of feet below. As adventurous passengers we would have all got out for a peek. Hell Gate was advertised as the most scenic spot on the entire Midland route and as one of the most scenic in America.

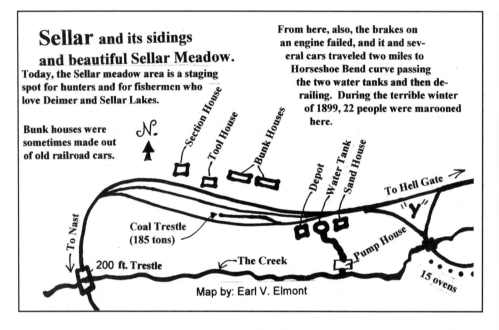

Sellar and its sidings and beautiful **Sellar Meadow.**

Today, the Sellar meadow area is a staging spot for hunters and for fishermen who love Deimer and Sellar Lakes.

Bunk houses were sometimes made out of old railroad cars.

From here, also, the brakes on an engine failed, and it and several cars traveled two miles to Horseshoe Bend curve passing the two water tanks and then derailing. During the terrible winter of 1899, 22 people were marooned here.

To Nast
Section House
Tool House
Bunk Houses
Depot
Water Tank
Sand House
To Hell Gate
"y"
Coal Trestle (185 tons)
200 ft. Trestle
The Creek
Pump House
15 ovens

Map by: Earl V. Elmont

Sellar was not a minor stop on the railroad, but not a major one either. It had conveniences, but no real town ever developed there. It was not as minor as Seven Castles that had only a water closet. Sellar had the second post office on the entire Frying Pan, pre-empted only by the little town of Calcium, later to become Thomasville. The first postmaster (never say "postmistress") was a Mrs. Rose Kirk. Seventeen other postmasters followed her at Sellar. Sellar had a couple of houses, a train station, a section house, a large water tank, a pump house, a couple of bunk houses, an inn, a sand house for making the tracks less slick in bad weather and for cleaning smoke stacks, some charcoal ovens and a big wye. Later, a round house replaced the wye for turning engines.

Sellar also had quite a few loggers. Perhaps that helped to make the meadow as bare as it is while all around is thick forest. A couple of the early settlers were Charles Isola and Harry Davis. Mr. Isola hired quite a few of the loggers.

Mallon Tunnel and the Chinese Village

The Mallon Tunnel cuts through a hillside about a mile or two below Hell Gate. Today the Frying Pan Road traverses the hill around the remains of the old railroad tunnel. Like most spots on the Frying Pan, Mallon Tunnel was named for an important railroad official. It was earlier called Hell Gate Tunnel, and in the numerical order of tunnels it is officially number 17. It was all dug by hand. No fancy hydraulic tools were used as were employed in the Hagerman and Busk-Ivanhoe Tunnels. The Mallon Tunnel was 448 feet long.

East entrance to the Mallon Tunnel.

Most certainly the Chinese men, who lived in a small village immediately above the tunnel, were among those who helped to build it. Six or eight dilapidated cabins still exist in the pine trees above the tunnel. Remains of two large horse barns still exist and a meadow where the horses grazed. There is a large mess hall that had three rooms: one for cooking, one for storage and one for eating. It appears

One of the larger cabins at the old Chinese village above the Mallon Tunnel.

that about twenty men could have eaten in there on one shift. Near the mess hall was a small ice house with double log walls filled with sawdust for insulation. The cabins appear to have had double occupancy and some possibly were for four men. All in all, it appears that from twenty to forty men lived in the little village

The rooftops were made of the flimsiest materials, so naturally they were the first to rot away. But the walls remain standing and make for a most interesting spot to visit. One can almost feel the spirits of those Chinese workers still existent among the trees today. On the northwest one can still find the access road that led up from the railroad to the village. Supplies reached the mess hall by this road. Mallon Creek ran right through the middle of the place. It is hard to believe, with our great fears today of giardia and other water-borne diseases, that they actually drank daily from that stream.

One can only venture a guess as to the number of deaths that may have occurred from these primitive living conditions. Speaking of deaths, no book has mentioned before, to our knowledge, that thirty Chinese workers allegedly perished from a massive cave-in inside the Busk-Ivanhoe Tunnel. Did the newspapers of the day cover the story and we moderns are just not aware of it? How do we know the tragedy actually happened? Well! Johnny Hyrup says it did and that he was told by his father Walt who was a railroad worker. So was Johnny's grandfather Jens Peter Hyrup, who was an engineer on the railroad. Those seem like pretty good sources. Johnny claims the bodies were removed from the tunnel and buried on the muddy shores of Lake Ivanhoe. In the making of the transcontinental railroads, Chinese lives appeared to be expendable. It is uncertain how many Chinese died in burrowing through the rugged Sierra Nevadas. It appears that their fate was hardly different on the Frying Pan route.

It is the author's guess that the Chinese did not live at the Mallon village

The old wagon supply road from the Chinese village at Mallon down to the railroad line.

very long. It appears to have been suitable for summer occupancy only. Because the construction of the rails moved so quickly, it is further doubtful that they lived there very long. There would have been no grazing for the horses, the creek probably would have frozen over and living in the cabins would have been miserable. If the D&RG went from Gilman in Eagle County clear to Glenwood in a year-and-a-half, then surely the Midland went down the Frying Pan quite rapidly. From all appearances the Chinese village was a temporary camp.

It is only in fairly modern times that the existence of the village was even known. It is believed that someone from the Forest Service discovered it. Certainly, an old-timer like Jim Crowley did not seem to know of it. Hunters may have used the cabins occasionally. Some of the tin cans out in the woods appear to be of fairly modern vintage. Other cans, especially in a massive pile near the mess hall, could have been from the Chinese occupants. Many of the Chinese were cooks in the construction camps.

Hell Gate

If ever a spot was well-named it was Hell Gate. It is not too distant from Lake Ivanhoe as one travels west. It is about a mile above the Mallon Tunnel. It was by far the most thrilling of all stops on the Colorado Midland Railroad. Everyone from Teddy Roosevelt, to movie actors, to musicians and famous photographers, to famous midgets, got out to look over the dangerous granite precipice. The more timid probably glanced from inside the safety of the train.

Hell Gate, once the most heralded stop on the entire Midland Railroad.

Huge granite outcroppings and giant boulder fields mark the spot today. The road is very narrow as it winds its way through cuts in the rock. As one looks downward from Hell Gate, he sees Ivanhoe Creek babbling its way several hundred feet below as it wends its way toward an eventual union with the Frying Pan River. One stands in sheer wonder at this spot trying to imagine how they ever made the cuts through such solid rock. One also wonders how many workers were injured or killed in the line of duty. One further imagines what many a winter storm must have been like at this spot. From the historical records we read of twenty-foot snow piles on top of the snowsheds. In the winter of 1899, as mentioned elsewhere, the snow was thirty-five feet deep.

Here and there at Hell Gate one sees rusting metal pipes sticking out of some of the bigger boulders. Though some think the pipes once held telegraph wires, in all the old photos the telegraph was supported by wooden poles, not

A splendid view from the upper end of Hell Gate looking west. In many places the end of ties extended to the edge of space. This is about where Victor Bigelow was killed in 1903 in a head-on collision.

metal ones. It is the author's opinion that these were drill bits intended to help split the rock that became entrapped and could not be extracted. Perhaps someone in the know could enlighten us. Higher up at Hagerman Tunnel, there are taller wooden poles that look like they may have once supported the telephone wires. We know for sure that Busk-Ivanhoe Tunnel had a telephone system on either end. There are some pretty sizeable power lines below Hell Gate. An older set of lines had to be removed by helicopter so the new ones could be installed.

As one gazes down the scary precipice, he sees large chunks of old rusty iron. On the left of the boulder field lie the remains of an old tender. This is the car that held the coal supply for the engine. That tender got down there when a landslide barely missed the engine and knocked the tender off the tracks. This must have greatly irritated the fireman. It is said that an attempt was once made to dynamite the tender so as not to frighten any passengers going by with scary tales. A huge piece of metal flew through the air and collapsed one support of a nearby electrical tower. No further attempts were made to demolish the tender.

Only Mother Nature is working on that job today. To the right of the tender, halfway down the hill, is an old Jeep. Don't ask how it got there!

Below the Jeep, and a little farther west, are the remains of an old Hupmobile. Darol Woolley of Basalt tells me that a Hupmobile was a forerunner to a Hudson. Here comes the story as told by Mr. Woolley: "A couple was coming west from Leadville in their Hupmobile. They had been drinking in the bars of Leadville. An argument ensued. The husband was drunk and abusive. The wife warned that he would come to no good. As she reached Hell Gate, a thought formed in her mind. She would 'give it the gas' and leap from the car onto the road bed. Hubby would never know what hit him." Now, the question I have is "Who told the story?" Perhaps the wife bragged all the way to Basalt. But wouldn't she be guilty of murder? I think I will insert an old adage at this point: "Better late at the Pearly Gates than to arrive in Hell (Gate) on time!" However the story happened, there IS an old Hupmobile down there today.

An old cabin once sat on the roadside on the east end of the most dangerous part of Hell Gate, where the trains always paused for a "look-see." It was the home of the line walker. It was his job to watch for big rocks on the track, loose rails, etc. Other old cabins existed down in the gorge for those who inspected the power lines. It must have been an awfully tough job in winter. One hiker told me he found a rusty old twenty-two rifle at the doorway to an old cabin right below Hell Gate.

Does the reader ever wonder how anyone survived the winters up the Pan in the old days? With the help of the trains, perhaps it wasn't so bad. One could hop over to Leadville or down to Basalt for supplies. Others could take a wagon on a sunny day to stores at Meredith, Thomasville or Norrie. The best prepared

Evidence of a former railroad siding near the Mallon Tunnel below Hell Gate.

families probably laid in some wild game and butchered some beef or pork. I can see the ladies making jams and jellies in warm weather. The author to this day makes chokecherry jelly each fall in the Basalt area. He has also made wild raspberry mixed with apple and other flavors.

The ladies did know how to can or bottle food in those days. I was amazed one time to hear an old couple tell me they bottled trout. I was further amazed to hear them say, that after removing the heads and tails and bottling them, the bones completely dissolved in the canning process. Wow! That was the most ticklish part about eating trout as I recall—those bones! Though the growing season was undoubtedly short, I am sure many old timers had gardens and raised chickens and rabbits. Many had fruit trees and knew how to bottle apple pie filling even. They would have stored salt, flour, sugar and other staples. They possibly even cured hams in a smoke house and made bacon. I guess "where there is a will, there is a way." But it still must have been tough.

How did they fight the flu and colds in the days before penicillin? (Old mustard plasters and night time walks in the chill air after bundling up the sick one very heavily). Many a soul met an early grave in those days and, sometimes, without so much as a decent marker. Such is the lot of my Noble and Hennings ancestors of Thomasville who are buried in a forgotten little spot above the road on the cast edge of Thomasville.

In August of 2002, Mr. Woolley and I met a most interesting young couple at Hell Gate. The only word to describe the obvious newlyweds was "cute." Mr. Woolley hadn't heard too much about Amish or Mennonites, but the author was quite familiar with them. He even knew that the Mennonites ran the main hospital in Glenwood. The author had visited their little rural villages in the heartland of America (Illinois, Iowa, Indiana, Pennsylvania and even Missouri).

The author visits with Mennonite newlyweds at Hell Gate. He gave the newlyweds a "tour" and had them taste their first wild raspberry.

He could tell by their conservative dress, especially the bride's, that they were Mennonites. After initial pleasantries, they proudly told us they were, indeed, Mennonites. The couple was very friendly and courteous. We immediately surmised that they were newlyweds. They had never seen wild raspberries. They were growing rather thickly on the edge of the road right at Hell Gate. The groom tried one. Normally they would have been larger and sweeter, but the severe drought had reduced them to something slightly less than tasty.

The groom asked if they dared take their little passenger car over Hagerman Pass. My brother and I had just gone over it to Leadville a week before. I had never been on such a wiggly-wobbly jiggly-jobbly ride in my life. I prayed that we would soon reach a paved road. We passed through giant cuts in snowbanks where the snow was two times taller than our pickup truck. We drove through water holes and over giant bumpy rocks in the road. Mr. Woolley and I both advised them not to risk the journey in less than a four-wheel drive truck or a Jeep. They took our advice.

I hope they eventually found a way to see Turquoise Lake and Leadville. I also wish they could have seen water flowing out of the Busk-Ivanhoe Tunnel's east end on its way to Pueblo and Aurora. As we left the handsome and whole-some young Mennonites, their video camera was "whirring." That would not be so with the Amish. They are not allowed any such modern devices. Instead of automobiles, they use horses and buggies. They cannot vacation on trains like the Mennonites either, though they are "cousins." Both groups were founded by former priests of a larger faith.

Ivanhoe Lake

I have always wondered if some Scottish person named Ivanhoe Lake. Whoever did it, picked a beautiful name. In the earliest photos it is identified as Loch Ivanhoe. That is the Scottish spelling.

Beautiful Lake Ivanhoe seen from Hagerman Pass.

I watched Grandma Newkirk pull some pretty nice fish out of the lake in the forties. It was my first visit to a lake so enchanting that I might as well have been on another planet. I was thrilled with the altitude and the fresh crisp mountain air. Grandmother could always outfish Grandpa Newkirk, her third husband. If he came home with three fish, grandma had five or six. She used a

Grandma Lydia Newkirk and her son, Fred G. Jakeman, Jr.

long cane pole. It almost looked home-made. When she fished near her ranch at Ruedi, she gave the line such a jerk that the fish flew clear up near her barn. She wasn't about to lose it. The little lady from Olewein, Iowa, met and married her first husband at Thomasville and homesteaded one-half mile above Meredith. When that husband (my mother's father) was killed, she married a Nelson and lived at Norrie and later on her ranch at Ruedi. When Mr. Nelson took off, she later married Forrest D. Newkirk who, according to Mr. Chris Jouflas, was the best fisherman on the entire Frying Pan. Apparently Chris never heard of grandma's fishing. Newkirk delivered the mail on the Frying Pan for years. A fisherman he was! They found him dead on the banks of the Frying Pan with his pole still in hand and his faithful dog King right by his side. King is etched on his tombstone.

Grandmother wasn't the only one who frequented Ivanhoe. I learned that Mr. and Mrs. Ray Jones lived and worked up there. Ray worked for the railroad and Jenny cooked for railroad workers. Later, my brother Walter and his friend Glen Kittle worked up there too. They worked maintaining various water supplies. They worked up there long after the Midland had gone.

Ivanhoe is such a beautiful lake. In the summer of 2002, we found out that the terrible drought had affected conditions even up that high. Their little "eternal spring" had gone completely dry. Workers had to truck in water, park the truck on the hill and let a large black gravity hose supply their water. The lake didn't look too bad so it must have had other inlets. In fairly modern times, a new dam was constructed. This caused the depth of the lake to increase and made what was once the approach to the

Looking west at the roadbed for the Colorado Midland Train just below the Busk-Ivanhoe Tunnel.

tunnel look like a "causeway." The newly-risen water found its way to the north side of the old railroad bed, giving some people a false impression of history. It is fun to walk down the newest approach and peer into the old tunnel entrance area. It must be done with permission. The roads in the area are still being altered today.

The workers in the little cabins were telling us how severe the winters can be up there. Even if no one lives up there in cold weather, they have to go in and plow the roads and periodically check on things. They say that the snow gets so deep that their equipment (snow cat) can drive over the top of a five-rung gate without realizing the gate is really there. They usually have to dig down in the snow four or five feet in the winter to find the top of the metal gate in order to open it and get into their cabins and work site. It didn't take long to realize the necessity of long snow poles with black tips sticking up on each side of the road.

Sleeping quarters and offices for the crew that keeps the water flowing from Ivanhoe through the Carlton Tunnel. Top of gate is five feet below snow in winter.

The Ivanhoe area is famous for thick rich peat moss. In the past, it was harvested and trucked out of the area. It is also at Ivanhoe where Mrs. Gina Terliamis and her children of Basalt and Sopris Creek used to run their sheep. It seems almost incredible that she walked her sheep all the way from Basalt. It must have taken weeks! How far can a sheep travel in one day? Don't they always stop to graze? As a child, in mother's car, I always hated to meet a herd of sheep (cattle too) along the way. It was always worse if the sheep were going the same direction as one's car. I was always afraid we would hit and kill one. I suggested to Darol Woolley that "....surely Mrs. Terliamis occasionally rode a horse or in a Jeep." "Nope," he replied. "Never!" When she passed his home at the Tucker McClure Ranch, she was always walking.

Her husband was Louis Terliamis, of Greek extraction. Their children were Nicky, Anna and Harry. I always liked the Terliamis family and their work ethic. Gina was Italian. Her mother, Mrs. Ermine Jorrioz of Basalt, was my favorite Italian outside of Aunt Linda. She was like a grandmother to my family. When her other husbands died, Mrs. Jorrioz married the hired hand Mr. Gene "Shorty" Chatrain. Shorty used to work for Phil Sterker up the Frying Pan at Castle View properties. Mrs. Jorrioz cooked for Shorty for years before she married him. When he knew Mrs. Jorrioz was cooking either polenta or "horse beans", he hurried up Tucker Hill as fast as his stiff leg would carry him. He raised the horse beans on his own property at the foot of Tucker Hill and she cooked them.

Mr. Terliamis raised goats as well as sheep. Goats ran wild up at the old Carl Adams Ranch east of Basalt high on the north hill. Larry Terrell and I found a couple and thought they were orphans. We carried them home in our arms. It was the coldest part of January. The little goats urinated down the fronts of our Levis and then it froze. We were most miserable when we got home. We tried to find a new home for these little orphans. Mr. Terliamis offered us 25¢ apiece for them. We did not realize what difficulties we probably caused for the mothers of the goats. They had been nursing the little babies. Suddenly they were gone. Oh, the foibles of youth! A little creek always ran right past Mr. Adam's house. I wonder if it is the source of Whitenack Falls today? Someday I must check it out.

Engine #2 in Ivanhoe Lake. The fireman jumped and swam out of the way.

For years I was confused by the tunnels at Lake Ivanhoe. I didn't realize at first that there were two of them, an upper and a lower. Now I know that the upper one was the Hagerman and was the first tunnel. The lower one was the Busk-Ivanhoe, later to become the Carlton Auto Tunnel. Due to its greater length and being closer to the water table, it was much more difficult to excavate than the upper one. All those who used to go through the Carlton Tunnel came out the other end wet and black with soot, especially if they were in a convertible.

Water still drips from the ceiling of the Hagerman Tunnel. Though the entrance is largely blocked, one can still wiggle his way in, but we don't recommend it after we tried it. Darol Woolley and his brother Larry and I entered the west end in the summer of 2002. Mr. Woolley had a large lantern attached to a car battery. We were amazed and excited at what we saw inside. We were halted by six or seven feet of ice cold water going back in for many feet. We could see beyond the water that the tunnel was clear. Wood

The old timbers supporting the tunnel entrance are as fresh and good as the day they were laid. The icy temperatures inside prevent them from decaying.

cribbing covered the walls and ceilings where the water was, but beyond that everything else was solid granite. Darol Woolley swears he is going in there someday with a boat. I asked him "What if you find a mountain lion's den?" He seemed unperturbed.

We were astonished at how well the cold water had preserved the tunnel timbering or cribbing. It looked like they had just been put in place yesterday. Only blackness from the smoke of countless engines had changed them from their earlier condition. We found the old sawmill site south and west of the tunnel where those timbers were cut and squared. Heaps of scrap wood lie in an ever-whitening pile bleached by the sun. The pile is at least 100 yards long, ten feet high and twenty feet wide. These were the round outside edges of the logs that would not serve for timbers. The timbers inside the tunnel are arranged in a most intricate pattern. What workers those former railroad men were! Each timber is of varying lengths and approximately twelve to fourteen inches thick. Here and there are lateral supports for those same timbers. The whole thing makes an upside down "U" shape and sits on a solid granite floor.

Bibliography

Abbott, Dan. *Colorado Midland Railway: Daylight through the Divide.*
Sundance Books, Ltd., 1989.

Cafky, Morris. *Colorado Midland.* World Press, 1965.

Danielson, Clarence and Ralph. *Basalt: Colorado Midland Town.* Pruett
Publishing Co., 1971.

McConnell, Robert H. *Colorado Midland Quarterly* 84 (November 2001).

McFarland, Edward M. "Mel". *The Midland Route: A Colorado Midland Guide
and Data Book.* Pruett Publlishing Co., 1980.

Nelson, Jim. *The Hot Springs Pool, Then and Now.* Blue Chicken One, 2000.

Roaring Fork Sunday Publications. *The Basalt Guide: Summer 1997.*

Shoemaker, Len. *Roaring Fork Valley: An Illustrated Chronicle.*3rd ed.
Sundance Ltd., 1973.

Index